ONLINE COUNSELLING

Online Counselling

A Handbook for Practitioners

Gill Jones
Anne Stokes

palgrave
macmillan

First published 2009 by
PALGRAVE MACMILLAN

Palgrave Macmillan in the UK is an imprint of Macmillan Publishers Limited,
registered in England, company number 785998, of Houndmills, Basingstoke,
Hampshire RG21 6XS.

Palgrave Macmillan in the US is a division of St Martin's Press LLC,
175 Fifth Avenue, New York, NY 10010.

Palgrave Macmillan is the global academic imprint of the above companies
and has companies and representatives throughout the world.

Palgrave® and Macmillan® are registered trademarks in the United States,
the United Kingdom, Europe and other countries.

ISBN-13: 978–0–230–20195–8
ISBN-10: 0–230–20195–4

This book is printed on paper suitable for recycling and made from fully
managed and sustained forest sources. Logging, pulping and manufacturing
processes are expected to conform to the environmental regulations of the
country of origin.

A catalogue record for this book is available from the British Library.

A catalog record for this book is available from the Library of Congress.

10 9 8 7 6 5 4 3 2 1
18 17 16 15 14 13 12 11 10 09

Printed and bound in China

This book is dedicated to the memory of the late Angela Burian,
without whom none of its content would have been possible.

Contents

Acknowledgements

We are grateful for the help and support of our friends, colleagues and students at Counselling Online Ltd who encouraged us to write this book. We particularly wish to thank the five people who read our early drafts – Kirstie Adamson, Janet Arbuthnot, Jacqui Atkinson, Roz Cawley and Jenny Womphrey. Their feedback and belief in this book were enormously helpful. Pauline Matthews and Alex Chew provided valuable input for Chapter 7, and Kirstie Adamson checked the English legal perspective in Chapter 11.

Lastly, and most importantly, we wish to thank our husbands, Bruce and Jonathan, for continuing to run the house, feed us and the animals, and not get too cross at midnight when we were still up white-water-rafting on the internet.

Foreword

We hope you will find this book useful, but before you begin reading, we thought it would be helpful to highlight some of the decisions we have made in writing it. This book is not a comprehensive reference guide to online counselling and technology. It is a handbook about online counselling, with text and exercises designed to give insight into and experience of some of the issues faced when working online. There is also a glossary at the beginning which may help with terms with which you are unfamiliar.

This book is intended not only for practitioners who wish to gain an insight into working as an online counsellor but also for those who have already begun to work online, or have undertaken basic training. It is not intended to replace training in this field, which we both feel strongly is necessary to become familiar with working therapeutically online.

We are both based in the UK and, although readers may come from many different parts of the world, we are using the UK English spelling system throughout except where technological terms require a different spelling (e.g. program). We use the term 'counsellor' to refer to anyone engaged in any of the psychological therapies. We hope this is acceptable to you, whatever term you use to refer to yourself. Predetermined genders for counsellors and clients have mainly been avoided, except where this did not make sense; in those instances, we used their real gender. Online counselling is above all about forming a relationship in which insight or change can take place. Parts of this book address the reader as 'you', and refer to the authors as 'I' or 'we', to reflect this relationship.

Both of us have worked as face-to-face counsellors for many years and have trained to Diploma level in online counselling. We are passionate about promoting online counselling and ensuring ethical practice in this field. Gill began working online in 2001, and Anne in 2002. Gill was a founder member of Online Training for Counsellors, while Anne joined the team in early 2003. This has been a pioneering organization, training counsellors to make the transition from face-to-face practice to working online.

We have drawn heavily on our experience as trainers to enable us to decide what to include that will be useful to people at all stages of involvement with online work. Our thanks are particularly due to those who read the first draft of the book as they represented the whole range – from someone who had done no online training to someone regularly working with online clients and supervisees. Their feedback has been immensely useful.

We hope you enjoy reading this book.

GILL JONES
ANNE STOKES

Glossary

Avatar   A graphic identity you either select from a group of choices or create on your own to represent yourself to the other party in a chat, instant messaging (IM) or multiplayer gaming session. An avatar is a caricature, not a realistic photo and can be a simple image or a bizarre fantasy figure.

Blogging   The practice of posting entries in your weblog. A weblog (usually shortened to blog, but occasionally spelt web log) is a web-based publication consisting primarily of periodic articles (normally in reverse chronological order).

Download   Collect data from a website e.g. a small computer program such as Instant Messenger.

Hardware   Objects that you can actually touch, such as disks, printers, computer screen, computer chips, audio headset, etc.

Internet   A worldwide network of computers that allows the 'sharing' or 'networking' of information at remote sites from other academic institutions, research institutes, private companies, government agencies and individuals.

Internet service provider (ISP)   The supplier of your internet connection (through your phone line) and provider of email address(es) and (often) some free web space for building websites.

Key drive   A portable storage device (usually small enough to fit on a key ring) which plugs into a USB port on your computer. Useful for storing confidential data such as session transcripts. Some key drives can be password protected.

Message board   A web application for holding discussions and posting user-generated content. Message boards are also commonly referred to as internet forums, web forums, discussion boards, discussion forums, bulletin boards, etc. Messages posted to message boards are displayed in chronological order or as threaded discussions under a common subject line.

Platform The underlying hardware or software for a system. The platform defines a standard around which a system can be developed.

Program Software placed on the computer to allow different methods of communication, e.g. email programs such as Outlook Express, Instant Messenger programs such as Windows Live Messenger, etc.

Search Engine A web server with a search facility, e.g. Google, Alta Vista, MSN, Yahoo!, etc.

Server A computer or device on a network that manages network resources. For example, a file server is a computer and storage device dedicated to storing files.

Software Computer instructions – anything that can be stored electronically is software, the storage devices and display devices are hardware.

Universal resource locator (URL) The unique address that web browsers use to find the web page you want, e.g. http://www.onlinetrainingfor-counsellors.co.uk.

Upload Send data to a website, e.g. send a large file to a web-server collection point such as www.pando.com or send your digital photographs to a website.

Video conferencing Communicating in real time with two or more people at different locations via video.

Virtual Reality An artificial environment created by computers in which people can immerse themselves and feel that this artificial reality really does exist.

Voice over Internet Protocol (VoIP) A category of hardware and software that enables people to use the internet as the transmission medium for telephone calls.

Web 2.0 A second generation of the web that focuses on the ability of people to collaborate and share information online. Web 2.0 refers to the transition from static HTML (HyperText Markup Language) Web pages to a more dynamic web that is more organized and is based on serving web applications to users.

Web browser or internet browser The program you open in order to surf the internet (e.g. Internet Explorer, Mozilla Firefox, etc.).

Webcam A camera that attaches to your computer and can be used to send either still or video pictures over the internet.

Web host Provides server space, web services and file maintenance for websites controlled by individuals or companies that do not have their own web servers.

Web server A computer that delivers (serves up) web pages to other computers.

Whiteboard A shared electronic workspace. Each participant can add text, make drawings or paste pictures on the whiteboard. Other participants can immediately see the result on their computer screen. Each participant can make a local printout or save the contents of the whiteboard to a disk file for later reference.

World Wide Web (the web) A client-server information system that uses the internet to access computers containing millions of hypertext documents.

Chapter 1

Introduction to Online Counselling

In this chapter we explore why clients and counsellors choose to work online. We examine some of the negative views that have developed as online counselling has spread in popularity, and we give a brief overview of how this form of counselling has developed over the years. It is important to say at this point that we do not see online therapy as better or worse than face-to-face (f2f) work – simply different. As this chapter introduces both online counselling and this book, we refer to other chapters that examine issues such as how to respond to emails, how to contract with clients and online supervision in greater detail. Finally, in Chapter 11, we consider how our ideas might be put into practice and attempt to identify new directions in which online counselling might be heading. This is a field where change is likely to be extremely rapid, and some methods of practice and the terminology may well become dated.

Various terms are used to describe the work of counsellors and therapists online: for example, e-therapy, online counselling, e-counselling and email counselling. We use all of these throughout the book to familiarize the reader with them all, and to avoid suggesting that one is better than another.

The terms describe the process by which counsellors and therapists use the power and convenience of the internet to help clients resolve their issues. Like f2f therapy, online counselling is a conversation or dialogue between two people, and the success of the work depends largely on the relationship that they are able to form. The counselling can take place through email exchanges (asynchronous communication) or simultaneous conversations in a chat room (synchronous communication). It can of course be a mixture of both.

Technologically, all that is needed is a computer that connects to the World Wide Web (the web), an email address, ways of ensuring privacy and confidentiality on the computer, and the skills to do this. Importantly, what is also needed is a working space that reflects good practice in engaging in a therapeutic relationship – e.g. lack of interruptions and distractions – and the mind set to ensure that the work is of as high a professional standard as if it were being undertaken in the client's physical presence. There is no room or excuse for bad practice, whatever the medium used.

WHY DO CLIENTS CHOOSE TO WORK ONLINE?

A myth is cited by Fenichel *et al.* (2002) that only people who cannot make relationships choose to work in this medium. This suggests that online work will not help the client, but rather reinforce the problem. However, our experience is that this is indeed a myth. The client range is as great as the range one might meet in an f2f consulting room.

Some clients choose this way of working because of their geographic circumstances. It enables them to engage in counselling if:

- they live in remote areas,
- they live in less remote areas, but where public transport is a problem, or
- few counsellors are available,

For others, there may be reasons why it is difficult to leave home, for example responsibility for care of the young, the old or the infirm. Those who work shifts, particularly when these have a variable pattern, may not be able to engage in regular f2f sessions.

Online counselling is also useful for clients with a disability. Those with mobility problems may have difficulties in accessing f2f premises, and/or difficulties with public transport. Those with hearing impairment may find e-counselling suitable, particularly where there is no access to a signer, or the nature of the issue means that the client prefers not to have a third person present in the room.

We have had a number of clients who regularly travel with their work and cannot commit to ongoing f2f sessions. Using email or instant messenger sessions, they can pursue their work and also engage in counselling.

In a few cases, clients may choose to work this way for emotional reasons. They may find it is easier to talk about shameful feelings or experiences online than face-to-face.

So far, it would seem that the reason for engaging in e-therapy is that access to f2f counselling is impossible. Metanoia's research paper on e-therapy states: 'the data seem to suggest that many of those who are drawn to contact a therapist on the Internet do so because, for them, traditional psychotherapy is not accessible' (http://www.metanoia.org/imhs/history.htm)

Our experience would again suggest that this notion that people only turn to online work if they cannot access f2f therapy is another myth, or perhaps an outdated concept. Increasingly, clients decide to engage in online counselling as a first choice. As use of the internet becomes more and more a part of daily life, many people regularly email and chat online to friends and family. They buy and bank online. The web is being used to access all types of information, and both computers and the internet are an integral part of the workplace. Thus using the internet for counselling does not seem to be such a difficult step to envisage. Many children use computers and the internet at school from a very young age, and so have few of the fears that older people may have about using them. In the UK, student counselling services are increasingly offering e-therapy as an alternative to f2f sessions. Cornell University in the USA is thought to have offered the first organizational online service in 1986 (http://www.cuinfo.cornell.edu/Dialogs/EZRA).

However, it should be rememberd that not everyone is enthusiastic about using the internet. Hudson (2002) suggests that poverty and a lack of technological training, as well as the fact that the older you are, the less likely you are to be comfortable with computers, are all reasons why some people may not use them. We expect this to change over time. Indeed, the growth in the number of internet users in Africa and the increasing use of it by 'silver surfers' worldwide suggest that this is already the case.

HISTORICAL OVERVIEW intro

At this point, it might be useful to give a short historical overview of online counselling. As many authors have cited (e.g. Fenichel *et al.*, 2002; Kanani and Regehr, 2003), non-f2f therapeutic work is by no means new.

Freud corresponded solely or partly with a number of clients which is worth bearing in mind when we question the possibility of engaging in any way other than face to face. At a more basic level, many of us have conducted relationships with friends and lovers through letters. Pen friends who have never met face to face will sometimes claim that they have established very close relationships. Therefore, perhaps after all there is nothing revolutionary about working relationally with text and image.

As far back as 1972, during a conference on Computer Communication, there was a demonstration of a simulated therapy session between computers in two American universities. Before that, there were software programs intended to be used to help patients, either alongside or instead of, work with a therapist. Perhaps the best known of these early programs was ELIZA, developed by the Massachusetts Institute of Technology. This was based on a person-centred means of responding. Although Weizenbaum, the originator of the system, did not see it as ever replacing the therapist and it ultimately proved unsuccessful, it was an interesting early development. Moving to 2007, WaysForward (http://www.waysforwards.com) have developed interactive programs that can be used by organizations or individual therapists with clients in schools, youth counselling services, universities and workplaces, but working from a solution-focussed brief therapy perspective. Hales (2006), who developed this software, reminds us such programs can sometimes seem too simplistic to counsellors, but that clients often find them helpful.

Since the mid-1990s, the Samaritans have been offering an email service alongside their perhaps better-known telephone service. Although the online service does not offer instant contact, which is available by telephone, it has become a well-established and well-used service.

Increasingly, student counselling services are finding that online counselling is a useful adjunct to f2f provision. This is possibly because internet communication is a daily part of students' experience, but also because students can access counselling while away from their universities and colleges on placements connected to their courses, or during vacation periods. They can also fit counselling around timetabled classes.

Particularly popular in the USA are websites that allow clients to access a counsellor directly for immediate help, or to post a message for an email response. These 'one-off' interventions can lead to an ongoing contract if the client chooses. Often these sites also offer information pages for visitors or clients on specific themes such as depression, stress, anxiety, or eating disorders.

Some organizations that were formed to help people with a particular issue, illness or disability have begun to offer an online counselling service alongside other support and information. Clients indicate to an administrator that they wish to engage in counselling and are allocated to a counsellor, who then makes contact with them. There is the opportunity to work either by email or through live chat. Whichever option the client chooses, the work takes place through the website, with clients and counsellors posting their emails to private message boards on the secure site. If live sessions are planned, a diary shows counsellor availability, which enables clients to book the session. This session also takes place through the website. This way of accessing counselling seems particularly appropriate for the client group, as it enables them to work when their illness or disability allows them to do so. They may also feel encouraged to engage with a counsellor who has some understanding of their illness and the issues that surround it.

Currently it would be fair to say that the volume of clients engaging in working online shows some marked differences across countries. In the USA and in Australia, it is more widely used than in the UK, for example. There is no research to suggest reasons for this. It may be due to the more recent introduction of training for online counsellors in the UK, and provision of online services. It could be that the use of the internet for other provision (such as for schooling in Australia) has made the population more ready to use it for other services, such as counselling. Perhaps it may simply be due to national characteristics – do people in the USA engage more readily in all forms of counselling than in the UK, for example? However, it is a counselling medium that is growing worldwide. Recent discussions have suggested that in some countries in Africa and Asia, where there has been a drive to provide more remote villages and areas with access to the web, there may also be a future increase in the use of internet-based counselling.

WHY MIGHT COUNSELLORS BE ATTRACTED TO ONLINE COUNSELLING?

So far, the discussion has centred on the reasons *clients* may choose to engage in online work. Why do counsellors choose to work in this medium? Probably there are as many reasons as there are counsellors working online. It may be that:

- they are curious about 'new ways' of working
- they wish to increase their client base
- they wish to use existing office skills in a different arena
- they want, altruistically, to make counselling available to as many people as possible, and the recognition that this is one way of doing so.

Perhaps there is also an awareness that this form of communication is here to stay, and if counsellors do not look at ways of joining the technological revolution, they may gradually become extinct like the dinosaur of old, or, less emotively, will not benefit from the opportunities it provides.

Counselling online also allows a certain amount of freedom that is not possible with f2f sessions. For example, Anne regularly spends time in France, and can continue to work with online clients, both by email and live sessions, when based there. (There are certain legal and professional indemnity issues with doing this that will be discussed later in the book.) At a simpler level, email responses can be written at times of day to suit ourselves. So if something crops up during a day, or during a week, as long as we remain within the contractual time of response, we can vary when we choose to work more easily than when we have set times to see f2f clients. In writing this, we are aware that we may be drawing disapproving comments from readers about commitment to clients, or to the profession. However, we would challenge you, if that was your immediate reaction, to think back to times when you have had to wrestle with a decision between going to an important meeting or interesting and useful workshop, and cancelling a client's f2f session. Online work often gives you the ability to do both.

'Carer' roles, disability and geographical location were cited as reasons that clients might consider this way of working, and these may apply equally to counsellors. While acknowledging that many counsellors do not enter the profession for economic reasons, but from a desire to enable people to live more effectively, or to resolve issues, nevertheless many of us also need or wish to earn a reasonable living. Working online, we are not limited by whether we can fit sessions around childcare provision, for example, or whether we can only take on clients with access to a car, as public transport does not fit around 50 minute sessions in our location. Counsellors with a hearing impairment may find that text based communication is a useful addition to other work.

Online counselling also offers practical advantages in that we can have all our work available to us to reflect on later. We can go back more easily to notice emerging themes, or spot nuances that we missed. In email exchanges, there is more time to consider what the client is actually saying, and how we might respond. These themes will be picked up again in more detail in the following chapters that deal with the nuts and bolts of working with clients.

WHY MIGHT COUNSELLORS CHOOSE *NOT* TO ENGAGE IN ONLINE WORK?

Perhaps the most common reason is a belief that online work simply does not work, and that a real relationship cannot be developed solely through text. Readers who have had 'pen friends' will be able to testify that very real relationships emerged, although they never met the other person. Indeed, although such relationships are often begun in childhood, there are numerous examples where they have been carried on successfully into adulthood. Maybe the sense that it cannot happen is a product of an age in which we write fewer letters of a personal nature, and forget that this was the preferred or only way of communicating in the past, before even telephones allowed more immediacy.

Another major concern is the technology itself. Is it safe? Is it reliable? The answer to both questions must be a qualified 'yes'. The practical considerations for making online counselling 'safe' and confidential for both clients and counsellors are dealt with in depth in later chapters, as are ways and means of working around occasional technological problems. As long as the counsellor can overcome fears of working with technology and become reasonably proficient in using it (as well as having quick access to support if needed) then using a computer to communicate can be relatively stress-free.

In addition, when considering absolutely valid questions of protection of client confidentiality and safety, it is worth reviewing our f2f work. Can we actually do more than give a qualified 'yes' here too? Even locked files can be broken into; if someone was really prepared to devote the time and energy to accessing our records or notes, could they work out the cross-referencing systems and discover who our clients are? Are we sure that all our walls are sufficiently soundproofed? Might clients be aware of who our other clients are because we work in an organization with a waiting room? What is being emphasized here is that no online counsellor can ever give a cast-iron guarantee that it is impossible for things to go wrong, and neither can an f2f counsellor.

So it does not appear that we are dismissing these concerns lightly, Anne relates how she came to be involved in online work.

> In early 2002, I was known as a 'luddite' by friends and colleagues. I did not actually smash computers, but might have liked to, and certainly refused, as far as possible, to have anything to do with them. The old tried and tested ways of communicating and gaining knowledge were the best for me. My counselling practice would never include anything to do with computers. Then a friend, who was undertaking training as an online counsellor, asked for volunteers to work as clients with other people in her training group. This seemed an ideal opportunity to confirm my prejudices – things would go wrong at a practical level if I tried to email a counsellor, and even if that did not happen, there was no way in which a therapeutic relationship would develop. As I write this, there is a vision of what a potentially nightmarish client I might have been, and not only because I was not expecting this to be useful. Although I do not recall being disinhibited when working online (for example when a client says much more than they may have intended to say very early on in a relationship), I know that I wrote very long emails to my poor counsellor. From my current position as an online counsellor, this was useful as it alerted me to the possible need to give some guidance on length of emails, or think about my charging policy. [These points will be discussed in more detail in Chapters 3 and 4, and also issues concerning boundaries in Chapter 11.]
>
> However, to my amazement, and also to my consternation, it was not quite like that. I managed the technology adequately, and did a very good piece of work with my counsellor on an issue that had been 'stuck' for some time. I had to reconsider where I stood, so began my own training, much to the amusement of my friends.

So for the counsellor who has doubts, perhaps a useful way of confirming or overcoming these might be first to become an online client. Then, if it is not for you, you have the experience to offer others. Check out the background of the counsellor before you do this – what are their qualifications, and are they trained in working online? As with f2f counselling, it is important to protect yourself as a client. If your experience as a client convinces you of the value of this way of working, and if you want to go further as a counsellor, it is advisable to undertake some form of training online. This has the advantage of allowing you to become more familiar with what is involved, and also to make mistakes and to discover or evolve your own style of working in a relatively safe environment. Most training courses are designed for counsellors who are already professionally qualified, so it is an additional rather than a first counselling qualification, although of course this could change in the future.

One other question often asked by counsellors wondering about working online is whether their particular orientation or approach will translate to this medium. We have yet to discover any counsellor who has been unable to do this. Chapter 9 explores a number of approaches in detail. The more cognitive theories adapt very easily as they generally use a rather more questioning than reflective approach. One common issue for counsellors from other approaches is how to rephrase online questions in the more reflective manner they use in f2f work. We hope our examples of counsellor responses throughout the book will demonstrate how we think this can be done. The tasks that a cognitive counsellor uses with clients between sessions are well suited to working online, as is the use of such techniques as scaling. Indeed, clients often find it easier to scale when they can actually see the grid on their screens than when introduced to it face to face.

Transference can and will arise online as it does in f2f work. If you undertake training in an online group that holds meetings in real time as part of the course, you will quickly be able to spot the possible transferences, counter-transferences and projections. They are also present in email communications. It is helpful to have experienced this before working with 'real' clients, as it can feel even more powerful when it is expressed through the written word.

Initially it may be difficult to envisage how you can use your more creative approaches online – with no stones, puppets, or drawing materials to hand. Chapter 7 explores many ways of using creativity. Clients may use creative writing, images they have found on the web, and images or photos they have created themselves and scanned in. In live work, it is possible to make use of a whiteboard to draw or write on during the session, depending on the package the counsellor uses.

In all approaches, difficulties may arise with a client who writes very little. This mirrors the f2f situation where the client is either temporarily or always somewhat inarticulate. In online work, this may feel harder to handle, as the counsellor cannot reflect back body language, for example, to try to help communication. Process can still be reflected back, of course, and the counsellor may also consider the benefit of using more but shorter email exchanges, or shorter live sessions. As in f2f counselling, some clients may find it just too difficult to engage, or are not yet ready to explore their issues.

An ethical as well as practical consideration for those contemplating working online with clients is the matter of supervision. This is discussed in detail in Chapter 8. If supervision is not mandatory for qualified counsellors in the country in which you work, you may not see this as a problem. However, in some ways, it can be akin to going back to basic training, where in most countries supervision is a requirement. Practitioners starting in this field may find that they want and need the back-up of a good supervisor. The question then arises of how to find a suitable one. Is it more important to work with someone who knows you and your work, and with whom you are already comfortable, or should you seek a supervisor who also works online and therefore has an understanding of the issues involved? In our view, there is no right answer. It may depend on whether you can find an online supervisor with whom you feel you can work. It does seem fundamental, however, to work with someone who is not antipathetic towards online work, even if they do not have the experience themselves, otherwise the supervision work feels doomed from the start.

This chapter has highlighted some of the issues involved in working online. In those that follow, we discuss these issues in more depth. You will be able to consider how to build a working alliance in this medium and how you might work both synchronously and asynchronously. Contracts, supervision, boundaries and ethical issues are explored, as well as how to work creatively using text and images. We also look at how therapeutic approaches may translate to online work, and other ways of using the internet for counselling. Before reading these chapters, you might like to try out some of the activities that given below.

Practice activities

I   Fill in the chart below concerning working online. As you go through the book, revisit this chart and see whether your hopes are upheld and your concerns diminished.

Hopes and expectations	Fears and concerns

2   Consider your current and past client group. Are there any clients with whom you feel you could work online? What would be the benefits for them? Are there any who would have been totally unsuitable? Note your reasons for both groups. Once you have finished reading the book, come back to this list and see if you would still place clients in the same groups.

3   What particular aspects of this chapter (for example the history, making therapeutic relationships, training) are you interested in? Research these further online.

Chapter 2

Making a Start

This chapter discusses and demonstrates how an appropriate relationship can begin to be built online. We look at some typical email enquiries and discuss what issues need to be clarified before contracting for the therapeutic part of the work can begin. For the purposes of this chapter we have assumed that you are ready to begin your practice as an online counsellor. We give some indications at the end of this chapter about how and where you might begin to have a presence on the web but we are not experts in website design or build and these aspects are not covered in this book.

You may have done some training specifically for online counselling or you may be hoping to pick it up as you go along. As you will have read in Chapter 1, training for online counsellors is available and we do urge everyone who wishes to work as an online counsellor to undergo it (see Chapter 11). Training will familiarize them with the online working environment and the technology they need. Your client may still be a technology 'newbie' who needs help and support from you just to make your communications work. If you are mystified by jargon words, see the Glossary at the beginning of this book; it covers all the words we didn't know when we began to work online. If we have missed any out, you can find definitions on the internet's own encyclopaedia, Wikipedia (http://www.wikipedia.com).

THE FIRST CONTACT

Initial enquiries from clients for online counselling generally arrive in counsellors' email inboxes. Once a new enquiry is received you will want to show the enquirer that you are competent to handle the issue they are bringing to you. This means that you will need to demonstrate you have understood both the issue and their feelings. You may also want to show them how you might work with them on the issue(s). However, before you can begin the work, you will need to check that you have understood them correctly, and during this process you will be beginning to build a relationship with them online.

We think it is very important to do this checking for understanding and preliminary relationship-building before you agree a basic contract (see next chapter) and engage with them therapeutically since the boundaries for counselling on the internet differ from those found in an f2f setting. The client has not moved out of their own environment to meet you; there has been no appointment to keep; they have simply written to you and sent you an email from their computer. Different types of supportive helping relationships on the internet can be found among the self-help websites, friendship websites, consultative websites and counselling websites, and you will need to clarify and distinguish your particular form of online relationship from all the others. From the beginning of any client contact it's important to explore any confusion that might be in the client's mind about whether you are offering them friendly support or you are both agreeing to engage in online therapy. Derrig-Palumbo and Zeine (2005) say 'the therapeutic alliance is initiated in the first session.' (p. 64).

Some counsellors question how and if trust is present online. We think that trust is present when both counsellor and client are communicating in a reliable, mutually agreed context, and clients feel they are heard and understood without being judged by their counsellor. Many people ask us about trust and how it is experienced online; we deal with this in other chapters as well as here. For example, Chapter 3 shows how contract-building develops trust through making an agreement about the limitations of the therapeutic relationship. Chapters 4 and 5 show how trust is built through both asynchronous and synchronous working alliances, and Chapter 10 shows how trust can be disrupted by boundary issues. We believe that for counselling to take place online, Carl Rogers's core conditions, cited in Thorne (1992), of psychological contact, empathy, genuineness and unconditional positive regard need to be present in the online relationship just as they are in the f2f one. We add warmth to this list, as some text communications have seemed to us terse, brusque, distant or cold; we do not think that such communications offer an appropriate relationship for working on painful, personal issues with a stranger whom you only experience through their words.

RECEIVING AND RESPONDING TO INITIAL ENQUIRY EMAILS

An initial email enquiry can be any length, with differing amounts of detail. We have received enquiries that are one line long and those that would run into more than a page. Here are some examples of initial enquiry emails.

- I've seen your website and I want to know how much you charge for online counselling. A
- I'm writing to you because I don't know where to turn. I'm so worried I can't eat or sleep and my head's just bursting with worry, I feel like I'm going crazy. Please can you help me? B
- I'm married to a man who doesn't want me. He spends all his time with his friend and never spends any time with me or our children. He puts him on a pedestal, almost worships him. If his friend says jump he asks how high. His friend doesn't like me because I speak my mind. He never takes holidays with the family he prefers to go away on lots of short trips with his friend. Do I call it a day? He says he doesn't need counselling. What can I do? C
- hi there I have been on your website today and would like some more information about online counselling i feel like I am very depressed at the moment and it is making me eat more so i put on weight and i am more miserable! This has been going on for a long time now and is causing so many problems in my life and in my relationship I recently married the man of my dreams and you would think things would be easier, but they are harder I am also usually so so positive and usually help others with their problems! i don't know wether you can help ? thanks so much and look forward to hearing from you. D

You can see from these examples that clients include very different amounts of information in their initial enquiry email. Some counsellors have an online enquiry form on their website which they invite clients to complete. This will normally include the type of information the counsellor requires to assess how to help the client therapeutically. But there is no guarantee that the client will use such a form, they may prefer to remain relatively anonymous at the beginning so that they can 'walk away' if necessary.

Practice activity

Write an email enquiry as a client and discover how much information you are comfortable disclosing about yourself to a stranger.

If you create a separate counselling email address at, say, hotmail or yahoo, you can send it to yourself.

COUNSELLOR RESPONSE TO INITIAL ENQUIRY EMAILS

At first glance you may be thinking that none of the enquiries above sound very promising client material, but we suggest that you don't know enough about them yet to make an assessment. If you are put off by the grammar and language, you might also be missing the sub-text of the message. Enquirer A might need to hear that you understand the risk they are taking if they disclose more information about themselves to you. Enquirer B might need some recognition by you of their immediate crisis and further exploration could lead to ongoing work or might end in a referral to a more appropriate service. Both C and D have entrusted you with some details about themselves, and you may want to explore the situation further with them, clarify your understanding of what they have written and introduce the idea of building an agreement to work together.

During these pre-contract email exchanges you are beginning to see if a reliable means of communication can be built which will form the basis of your counselling relationship. You are also assessing whether or not you can work therapeutically with this client within the code of your professional body. The International Society for Mental Health Online (ISMHO) has produced a useful online paper about assessment of client suitability for online work (see References for website address). There are several issues for you to consider at this point some of which are listed below:

■ Do you understand both the surface- and the sub-text of the writing (check for understanding during the pre-contract stage).
■ Are the issues presented so far ones that you feel competent to work

with online? Are they familiar to you (perhaps from your f2f practice)? and do you feel they are appropriate for online work?

■ Are there any special issues (cultural, geographical, medical) that might also need to be taken into account here?

Your reply will contain a tentative summary of the situation and your understanding. It should also indicate that you could be wrong and are happy to be corrected. In addition, your reply should show your empathic understanding of what the client might be feeling; in our experience, unless you can engage empathically with potential online clients, they are unlikely to continue contacting you. This reply to their initial enquiry is an opportunity for you to show them that you have understood them at a deep level. In reply to Enquirer A you may want to show that you understand they could be finding it difficult to write about themselves.

Your reply might be:

> Hello A, Thank you for choosing my website and writing to enquire about some online counselling and its costs. It's sometimes hard to write about yourself to a complete stranger and to click the Send button. I have pasted my costs below this email and you can also find them at www.gjcounselling.co.uk/pages/counsellingcost.htm. Please write to me again if you have any further questions. If you do contact me again perhaps you will feel able to write a little bit about yourself and the situation you are facing at the moment. I look forward to hearing more from you when you are ready. Warm regards, Gill Jones

In contrast, in a reply to Enquirer C you may want to describe your own particular way of working online or to make some suggestion about the focus of the counselling.

> Hello C, Thank you for choosing to write to me about the situation you are facing at the moment. I sense you are feeling angry and rejected by your husband's preference for the company of his friend to you. Perhaps you also feel he's letting you and your children down by not being there. Please let me know if I've misunderstood anything – it's easy to misunderstand when we've only got words to go on. I think online counselling might be a useful space for you to explore these strong feelings and hopefully we can together find a way for you to deal with them. If you would like to go ahead and do some therapy with me, it is important we

have an agreement in place which says how and when we are going to communicate and whether we will be using email or live sessions, so I'm attaching here my basic agreement which we can adapt to suit ourselves. Please ask me any questions you want to before completing your part and returning it to me. Once the agreement is complete, we can begin the work. I look forward to hearing more from you when you are ready. Warm regards, Gill Jones.

Any response to an initial enquiry will need to demonstrate warmth, genuineness, empathy, unconditional positive regard and psychological contact to establish an appropriate working relationship. If you have a pre-counselling questionnaire or mood inventory on your website which a new client has completed and sent to you, your first email contact will also include an acknowledgement of this information.

Your personal writing style should convey your meaning clearly and concisely. You may need to adapt and simplify your language, avoid jargon or long, obscure words and keep sentences short and simple. Brief enquiries need brief responses if possible as there may be reasons why the enquirer has kept their email brief (they may have a disability which makes typing and reading difficult or they may be writing in their second language). You may also want to check at an early stage the ease with which the client can undertake the therapeutic work alone and uninterrupted. Privacy and confidentiality of email counselling are important issues to consider before any therapeutic work begins; they are discussed in Chapter 4.

How you begin and end your emails is personal to you. Many counsellors prefer to use Hello or Hi rather than Dear in the greeting line. This follows the majority of email greetings and distinguishes them from postal letters. Most online counsellors address clients by name, even if the only name you have is an incomprehensible part their email address such as funnyface, bigeyes or f61 (it can prompt the enquirer to add a name to their next email). It is good manners to thank them for choosing to contact you from among the thousands of counselling websites, and it gives you an opportunity to affirm them for taking the initial step towards getting some help for themselves. As we have mentioned above, your reply should also contain a sentence that shows what you have understood of their feelings even when that understanding is offered tentatively. It is validating for the client and most important if you don't want them to walk away feeling unheard and misunderstood. If you have a sufficient description of the issues the client wants to bring, you may want to include your contract or agreement with your reply, inviting them to read it through and discuss it with you before completing their part. Discussion helps to involve and engage them in the task ahead. How you end the email is again a matter of personal preference. Many online counsellors use a favourite ending phrase which appeals to them such as 'warm regards' or 'warm wishes', and many counsellors use the signature box in their email program for a meaningful quotation which follows their name on every email. For example, you might end an email by saying

Warm regards,
Gill Jones

Trouble is part of your life, and if you don't share it, you don't give the person who loves you a chance to love you enough (Dinah Shore)

This is a useful way of personalizing the email and showing it has come from you.

If you need further information from the client before deciding whether or not you might be able to work together, obtain this without inviting an inappropriately detailed description of their issues in their next email (see response to Enquirer A). If you subsequently feel you are not the right counsellor for them and suggest they try someone else, they should not be left feeling exposed and vulnerable as well as rejected by their experience with you.

Practice activity

Write an initial response to Enquirers B and/or D

Suggestions for responding to an initial enquiry

- Use their name in the greeting – thank them for choosing to write to you
- Affirm their decision in writing (they're doing something about the situation)
- Empathize with their feelings
- Introduce a form of contract (if this seems appropriate at this stage)
- Check for understanding and invite them to correct you
- Avoid assumptions – keep observations/thoughts tentative
- Be warm, empathic and genuine, and offer unconditional positive regard
- End with personal choice of phrase

BUILDING A RELATIONSHIP USING TEXT ONLY

How do we build a relationship with someone we can't see or hear? What alternatives are there for the non-verbal cues that are so informative to a client/counsellor relationship in the room? As this book is mainly concerned with communication from a computer keyboard (rather than webcam or internet phone), this chapter will explore the different ways a relationship is built within these limitations.

Before any emails have been written, most potential clients will have formed an impression of you, the counsellor. They have decided to contact you after reading about you either on your website or in an online directory. A few will have contacted you because someone else has recommended you to them (e.g. a past client). It is likely that they chose to make contact with you because of what they read and may well have formed a picture of you from what they have understood about you so far. This is advantageous for you (their chosen counsellor) because it means they already have a positive response to your words and the relationship 'fit' is likely to be a good one. Of course, the reverse can also be true: your reply may not fit their expectations, in which case you probably won't hear from them again.

In the same way you will build an impression of the writer from the text of their enquiry email. You will respond to how they use words and phrases, punctuation marks, layout and keyboard characters to convey thoughts and feelings. Here are two examples of words with different punctuation. Do they convey the same feelings to you?

1 after work we meet at the supermarket, she chooses all that she wants and we get to the till and she just looks at me saying well i dont have money with me, ahh man, was i f...... off

2 after work we meet at the supermarket, she chooses all that SHE wants and we get to the till and she just looks at ME saying well i don't have money with me, ahh man, was i F...... OFF!!!

Some clients may use keyboard strokes such as :-) or ;-) (smile or wink) or put feelings inside angle brackets such as <grin> <sigh> to express how they are feeling as they write; or they may use emoticons like these 😊 😔, which are often used during live chat sessions (see Chapter 5 for more details). Most online counsellors will wait for the client to take the lead and not introduce these elements into the dialogue themselves as some clients can find them off-putting, seeing them as simplistic, lightweight representations of complex and often painful feelings. However, this isn't always the case, as Fenichel *et al.*, (2002) state:

> Experienced e-mail users have developed a variety of keyboard techniques to overcome some of the limitations of typed text – techniques that almost lend a vocal and kinesthetic quality to the message. They attempt to make e-mail conversations less like postal letters and more like a face-to-face encounter. Some of these strategies include the use of emoticons, parenthetical expressions that convey body language or 'sub vocal' thoughts and feelings (sigh), voice accentuation via the use of CAPS and *asterisks*, and trailers . . . . to indicate a transition in thought or speech. Use of 'smileys' and other commonly used symbols can convey not only facial expression but also a variety of emotional nuances. When used sensitively, emoticons can be an effective, subtle and eloquent way of expressing feelings which belong in the 'here and now' relationship you have with your client.'

Familiarity with mobile phone text shorthand is also helpful for online counsellors as some clients use this freely in their emails. For example, how do you want to respond to text that looks like this?

> I finlly got ur email . . . Nyways . . . I dont want my parents to get upset if they fnd out abt this . . . thats y I didnt want 2 giv u my phone no.!

ADDING INTERPRETATION TO THE WORDS

Online counsellors are aware of how differences in visual impact (the use of font, colour, language and punctuation) can affect their interpretation and understanding of what's been written. However, these differences are not visible if their email program is set to Plain Text and not Rich Text, or they copy and paste the text of the email into a Word document and neutralize the formatting (layout). They are also aware that their client's email program may also be set to Plain Text, so online counsellors keep their email replies neutral and if formatting is desirable, may send this as a Word document attached to an email.

As well as these differences, there is a second, more important, way in which people respond to the words they read. When we are reading, most of us are hearing the text as spoken words in our head and this is already interpreting what we read. In order to make sense of text, we are adding our choice of inflection (emphasis and tone of voice) and pace (how fast the words are being spoken, where to put a pause). This interpretation is unavoidable unless we 'hear' the words as a monotone, without any inflection or pause (most of us don't do this).

Online counsellors and their clients are interpreting what the other has written right from the beginning, and there is a significant potential for misunderstanding. At the initial enquiry stage (when neither knows much about the other) the online counsellor's interpretation of the client's words may not be accurate and the counsellor invites the client to correct them. It's important to establish that misunderstandings can happen (particularly at the beginning) and that both of you expect the other to correct any misunderstandings as soon as they are noticed. A mutual arrangement like this builds trust and helps to create a working alliance based on equality rather than authority. It can be incorporated quite easily into a response (see counsellor response to Enquirer C).

Sometimes a client's email address is 'informative' in ways that might cause you to judge them before you have begun counselling. Here are some slightly altered email addresses of real counselling clients. How would you feel about counselling someone whose email address was lickylips@googlemail.com or greasyjo@yahoo.com? And what might you deduce about this email address chrisandjane@hotmail.com?

Practice activity

Imagine you are working online as a counsellor for a general counselling agency which offers both f2f and online counselling. How would you respond to this initial email enquiry? (Remember: you don't know if they live locally)

> Hi, I saw your website and thought you might be able to help me. I have panic attacks and I'm frightened to go out of the house now, unless someone is with me. I've been like this for a long time and I'm fed up with it. Do you think you can help me?   Mary

SETTING UP YOUR ONLINE COUNSELLING SERVICE – TOOLS

What tools do you need to work online? Here's a basic checklist.

1   *Your computer*   This should be relatively new (less than three years old), with plenty of memory. It doesn't matter if it's a laptop or a desktop, but it should have adequate password protection – e.g. it asks for your password every time you start up from hibernation as well as every time you switch on. If you can't password your computer you could store your confidential client work on a removable storage disk which can be locked in a filing cabinet. A USB or key drive (see Glossary) is ideal. Laptops are easy to carry around with you and to put away, so the worktop can be used for something else. But they can also be easily stolen; desktop computers are less easy to steal but take up space permanently.

2   *Internet connection*   You buy this from an internet service provider (ISP) such as AOL, Freeserve, BT Openworld, Virgin Media, Dialpipex, Sky and many others.

3   *Web browser*   You will need web browser software in order to access the internet (e.g. Microsoft Internet Explorer, Mozilla Firefox, Safari, etc.). Many computers come with web browsers already loaded.

4   *Email program and email address*   You will need email software (e.g. Microsoft Outlook, Outlook Express, Mozilla Thunderbird, Mac Mail, Eudora) which some computer dealers pre-load, and an email address. Your ISP will give you one email address (joe.bloggs@virgin. net) when you sign on, which you might want to keep for personal emails. It is sensible to have a second email address for work – this could be another address with your ISP (counselling@virgin.net) or an email address with a remote web-server such as hotmail or yahoo (joebloggscounselling@hotmail.com). The benefit of having access to your email from a remote web-server is that you can access your emails from any computer; if you are storing them on a USB drive, your client work can travel with you and take up very little space.

5   *Anti-virus software* (such as Norton, McAfee, AVG, etc.) which is updated frequently (daily if possible) to ensure that your computer neither becomes infected by a virus from your client's computer, nor passes on a virus to theirs.

SETTING UP YOUR ONLINE COUNSELLING SERVICE – PROFESSIONAL REQUIREMENTS

The list below is only basic; the topic is covered more fully in Chapter 11.

1   Professional indemnity insurance – check with your existing insurance provider about any limitations and restrictions they place on internet clients who live abroad.
2   You may also want to register with your government as a keeper of sensitive data since the work you will be doing will be held on your computer (even temporarily). UK clients can check online to see if you are listed on the Data Protection Register (for UK information visit www.ico.gov.uk).
3   Professional associations and support. Make sure the professional body you are affiliated to (e.g. BACP, BPS, UKCP, etc.) understands and supports your online work. If they hold an online register of their members, clients can find you there and see that you are who you claim to be.
4   Consider joining a professional association that specializes in support-ing counsellors who work online, e.g. Association for Counselling and Therapy Online (ACTO), website www.acto-uk.org, and the International Society for Mental Health Online (ISMHO), www.ismho.org. They offer you contact with other online counsellors and discussion forums on professional issues of mutual interest.
5   Check the requirements of different Codes of Practice relating to online therapy (see Appendix).

PUTTING YOUR ONLINE COUNSELLING SERVICE ON THE INTERNET

Where can you advertise your online counselling service? You could advertise in places where you know your f2f clients will find you (e.g. GP practice, local press, library, etc.), but you may only attract clients who might prefer to have f2f sessions. Working online could bring enquiries from anywhere in the world, and it's this type of advertising we are consid-ering here.

Here are some suggestions.

■ Place an entry in a website directory of counsellors (such as www.bacp.co.uk, www.onlineclinics.com, www.acto-uk.org or www.mytherapynet.com). This will usually cost money but some directories will have good facilities for providing confidential chat and message spaces plus automatic billing of clients. The more popular websites will have many visitors, which increases the likelihood of your entry being seen. The drawback (apart from the cost) is that you are one among hundreds of other counsellors and you might not be noticed by a potential client.

> **Tip**
> Check how easily a website is found by searching for it using different search engines (Google, Yahoo, MSN, etc.). Put words you would use if you wanted to find a counsellor into the search boxes (eg depression counsellor; online counsellor; counselling for anxiety; panic attack counselling; PTSD counselling, etc.). Websites that appear on the first page of results will be viewed by the largest number of people.

■ Join with some like-minded colleagues and collaborate on creating a website in which you each have a personal web page. In this arrangement you get more space to describe yourself and your service (some large website directories limit individual descriptions to just a few words). You and your colleagues share any costs for getting your website on the internet.

■ Create your own website in which you describe yourself and your service in as many web pages as you like. Then, if you don't mind having a complicated web address which people might find difficult to remember, such as http://freespace.virgin.net/joe.bloggs, you can upload your website files to the free space provided for you by your ISP. If, however, you prefer to have a simpler and more memorable website address such as http://joebloggs.net, you will need to acquire and register a domain name (the bit after http://) with one of the domain name registration websites. Then you are ready to upload your files to a web host (see Glossary). Web hosts such as 123-reg.co.uk or bravenet.com simplify the process of creating your own website by having a series of website templates where you can add your own content and then upload everything to their web server (see Glossary). They also handle domain name registration. Domain name registration and web hosting cost money, but prices vary widely and you should research which one best fits your pocket.

■ Ask a friend who is already a knowledgeable internet user to help you do the complicated tasks of registering a domain and uploading your website, leaving you to concentrate on the content of the web pages.

■ Once your website is on the internet it will need to be found by the search engines. You can perform this process (known as search engine optimization – SEO) once you know how, but there are also many websites offering search engine optimization (for a fee). Some web hosts have online tutorials on search engine optimization (take a look at http://webceo.com or try searching on the search engines for SEO tools).

Practice activity

Visit both directory and individual websites for counsellors and note what information is there. Plan how you would describe your counselling service. What information would you include?

In this chapter we have considered how an online counselling relationship begins and what considerations might be important for creating a counselling presence online. In Chapter 3 we show you how to develop and negotiate a mutually agreed counselling contract with your client (so the therapy may begin). Anyone working for an organization offering an online counselling service may already have a pre-set contract and think the next chapter is unnecessary, but we advise them to read through it anyway in case some incidental details are missing from their existing contract. They might want to negotiate these with their online clients.

Chapter 3

The Online Contract

INTRODUCTION

Online contracts form the secure basis for all therapeutic work. Crouch (1997) states that a professional structure holds the framework of counselling together, and that one of the requirements for this is a clear agreement with the client about the counselling. Given that premise, this chapter will encourage you to consider various aspects of contracting, and how your current f2f contract may need to be adapted for online work. Counsellors do not necessarily have a written contract for f2f counselling, but the very nature of online work makes it absolutely necessary to have this in a written form to send to clients. Some of the therapeutic issues and ethical issues are dealt with in other chapters, so here the concentration will be on the content of the contract and various ways of contracting with clients.

According to Chechele and Stofle (2003), online counsellors need to address several 'housekeeping' issues before beginning therapeutic work, including informed consent. So however keen the client is to get into the work, the counsellor's task is to ensure that the preliminaries are completed.

The initial enquiry from the client will usually be through an email, and may well contain quite a lot of information about themselves and the issue(s) they wish to bring to counselling. While not ignoring this, the counsellor should, in responding, focus on contracting details, rather than beginning the counselling process. The same skills are needed as are employed when receiving a telephone call from a prospective client. They may want to tell the counsellor a great deal about their issue, while the counsellor wants to make sure that the telephone call itself does not turn into a mini-counselling session.

INITIAL EMAILS AND RESPONSES

We have already looked at initial enquiries in Chapter 2, although the focus there was on building the therapeutic alliance. Here we use examples of very different initial emails received in order to consider the online contract.

> I have looked at your website and wish to have some counselling with you. Can you help me? Sam

> Dear Anne,
> I've been looking on the internet and found your name. I want to sort out my life as it feels a mess at the moment. My partner has said he is going to leave me if I don't get a grip. My children are driving me stark staring bonkers, and my mother is really being difficult. I've tried talking to friends but they all give me different advice. It's like being in a sandstorm. Some say I should just batten down the hatches and weather the storm as it will all go away. Others say I should leave my husband before he leaves me. And some say I am making a mountain out of a mole hill. It's all affecting my work, my social life and my family life. I just don't know what to do. I go from being an angry buzzing bee all the time, to being in floods of tears, and I don't like the children seeing me in either of those states. Even worse in a way are the times when I just feel numb and don't really care what happens to me or the family. It's affecting everyone. My oldest kid is taking exams this year, my friends must be sick of me whining on, and at times my husband and I barely talk.
> Can you suggest what I should do?
> Jo

In the first example, it might appear easier to contract with the client as there is little to respond to therapeutically, so the business aspects can be explored. However, there is also little to inform the counsellor about whether this is a client with whom they feel it will be possible to work – what is the issue for counselling? Is it suitable for online work? Does it fall within the areas in which the counsellor chooses to work? At this point, you do not even know if 'Sam' is male or female.

In the second example, the skill will be to ensure that the client feels heard and is held therapeutically while the contract is put in place. This is a difficult balance to achieve, and counsellors will have their own ways of responding, depending on how they work and their personal style. The examples of responses given below should therefore not be taken as correct models, but simply as possible ways forward. You will need to formulate your own responses that feel comfortable for you.

> Dear Sam,
> Thank you for contacting me. So that you know how counselling online works, I am attaching my contract for you to read. This gives practical details about ways of working, fees etc. It is possible that you've picked up some of this information from the website, but it's important that we are clear about details before we begin, so that we can then leave these aside and concentrate on what it is you would like to work on. If anything isn't clear, or you feel that something has been left out of the contract, please do tell me.
>
> Once you have read the contract, if you would like to begin counselling with me, would you please email it back to me with the information about you filled in. Maybe at the same time, if you don't have any queries which need answering at this point, you would like to tell me something about the issue you would like us to work on. I work with a range of issues, as you'll have read on the website, but if it seems that I would not be the best person to help you, I will give you the names of some other counsellors who also work online.
>
> I hope this information is helpful and doesn't seem too much at the moment. I am looking forward to hearing back from you, Sam, and hope we can work together.
> Warm wishes,
> Anne

This is a much longer reply than Sam's initial query, and could set up an expectation that the counsellor will always write more than is received, but that can be dealt with in later emails if necessary, if the contract is set up.

In responding to the second example, the counsellor needs to touch on the issues, but not invite back too much more therapeutically, in part to protect the client if the work does not go ahead. If the client begins the work before agreeing to the contract, and for some reason the work does not go ahead, Jo could be left feeling exposed and vulnerable. Of course, it does happen that a client who has 'offloaded' in an initial email may actually have done what they needed to do, and may not wish or need to go further. That can be frustrating for the counsellor, who has spent time carefully trying to get the reply right, but in some ways this is no different from initial telephone contacts that do not develop into an appointment.

A possible reply to Jo is shown below:

> Dear Jo,
> Thank you for contacting me. It sounds as if you are finding things really difficult at the moment and that you don't know how to go forward, as all parts of your life are being affected. That must be hard for you, and I can hear how you're experiencing a whole range of emotions.
>
> I hope that we can work together to help you discover how you can change the situation and so I am going to attach my contract to this email. Once you have read it, there may be questions you want to ask about it, so please feel free to do so – it's important that we get it right at this point so we can then concentrate on working together. You'll notice that I also ask for some factual information about you. This is so I don't have to keep asking you for details later.
>
> I'll look forward to hearing from you again, Jo, when you return the contract. As I read through your email, I was struck by your ability to use images to vividly describe how you were feeling when you wrote. If you decide to work with me, maybe we can explore some of these.
> With warm wishes,
> Anne

Jo's request that the counsellor suggests what she should do has not been picked up, though the reply does state that Anne will 'help you discover how you can change the situation.' The contract may need to emphasize that the counsellor does not give advice or tell clients what to do. Rather than stating baldly that therapeutic emails will not begin until a contract has been agreed, the reply tries to discourage too much more in this vein by using the phrases 'it's important that we get it right at this point so we can *then* concentrate on working together' and 'from you again, Jo, *when* you return the contract'.

One thing these initial responses do not state is by when the counsellor expects to hear back. Not stating that you would like to hear back within a week, or two weeks, can leave you in limbo, as you try to plan your work and accept new clients. Will this one materialize or not? Have you the space to accept any other client who then contacts you? However, at this point, you may not want to appear to be pressurizing the client into making a decision; they may need time to reflect. There is no simple solution to this; if you have only one space left to accept a new client, for example, you may decide to say that you would like to know within a certain time that they want to work with you, and perhaps be upfront about the reason for this.

Having told the client that you are attaching a contract, it may be stating the obvious to say that this needs to have been prepared before you ever receive your first request for online counselling. However, sometimes counsellors have been so busy concentrating on considering how they will actually carry out the therapeutic work that they have not prepared a contract. If you have a standard contract ready on your system, you can send it at once, or perhaps first adapt it, for this particular client.

Ideas for items to be included in a contract
(in no particular order of importance)

- Ways of working together (synchronously or asynchronously)
- Fees and how to pay them
- Information about yourself
- Professional information such as the Code of Practice you work to
- Arrangements for breakdown of technology
- Arrangements for unplanned endings
- Confidentiality
- Security online
- Request for personal information
- Timing of exchanges of emails or sessions
- The difference between therapeutic and non-therapeutic emails
- Limits to the amount a counsellor expects to receive in any one email
- Personal crisis procedures
- Supervision information

You may feel overwhelmed at this point by questions of how to get in all you need to without making the document too long for the client to read and take in, and be tempted to include just a few basic points. A balance needs to be struck between what items are essential for you to include, and what you can risk leaving out without causing problems later on if they have to be added. For example, it is too late to discuss what to do if a computer crashes if it has already happened. On the other hand, you may decide not to include information about yourself, as this can be read on your website.

If possible, the language you use should be appropriately professional, and also reflect something of you and the way you work. This is much harder to achieve online than face to face, as you cannot 'soften' the language as you might when going through a written contract with a client in your counselling room. You cannot judge their reactions, and pick up what has been misunderstood or has caused them concern. It is worth asking friends or colleagues to read through your contract, making any changes in light of their responses before using it with a client. If you choose routinely to evaluate your work with online clients, you could also include a question about how they reacted to your contract documentation. Some of the suggestions for inclusion in a contract are revisited in later chapters.

CONTRACT FOR ONLINE COUNSELLING

Bayne *et al.*, (1998) suggest that a contract commonly includes two elements: one concerned with your approach and the other with practical arrangements and conditions. You will probably want to begin with a general statement that gives a little background about yourself. If you have a website, refer to it, so that you do not need to make this document so wordy. An example might be:

> Introduction
> I am a registered practitioner with (name of professional body), and work to their Ethical Framework. You may be interested to know more about this and can find it on their website at http://......... You can also find out more about my background on http://............

The next section deals with fees and session timings. You may choose to put this in later if you feel that it is too business-like to look immediately at this aspect of the work. We put it here because if the client does not wish to meet our fees, or does not like our timing suggestions, we would rather not waste their time in reading through the rest. In addition, this is a professional business arrangement, which will then give the safety for the therapeutic work, so these arrangements have to be agreed upfront.

> ### Fees and times
>
> The fees are .... per email exchange, or .... per Messenger session (up to one hour). You can pay through an online payment system such as PayPal, by UK cheque, or by bank transfer. Many clients prefer to pay in a 4 exchange block ahead of our communications rather than paying for each individual exchange as we go along.
>
> I suggest that initially we agree to work together for 4 live sessions or 4 email exchanges, whichever would work best for you. Messenger is an alternative to email exchanges, where we are able to use weekly sessions to talk in 'real time' on a screen if you wish to do so. Sessions would be up to an hour long. This is something we can discuss together in these initial emails, if you are not clear about how this works. After that, we will review how the work is helping you and whether you wish to continue. You can send me emails on whatever day of the week suits you, but I will only respond therapeutically to them on Tuesdays, as this is my day for working online. I will number my responses as Therapeutic email 1, 2, etc, and send them as an attachment, with a short covering email message.
>
> I will email you an acknowledgement that I have received emails. It would also be useful if you would also acknowledge my emails, then we know that the technology is working.

The example given above allows counsellors to plan their week in terms of when they will respond, and we found it to be appropriate when we began working online. As they become experienced in working online, some people prefer to be more flexible about the way they work. They do not mind if they receive a number of emails from a client within a week, even if they will not necessarily reply to them individually. We would not recommend this if you are setting out as an online counsellor, as it can feel overwhelming. It is more manageable, boundaried and structured to keep to a set time for your responses.

However, if you are already experienced online, and if your practice is not to have a set day of the week when you see a particular client, you might write something like this:

If we are working by email, you can send me emails when you wish, although I can only guarantee to respond to them within three working days (excluding weekends). That means that if you send several close together, you may find that I reply to them all in one email. I will number my responses as Therapeutic email 1, 2, etc, and send them as an attachment, with a short covering email message.

You may also wish to put in a paragraph about what happens if the client experiences a crisis. Some counsellors feel that when working online it is very difficult to give support at such times. Others feel that it is essential to offer this. Your response may be governed by what you would be able, and are prepared, to offer to f2f clients. In this case, you would try to find a way of offering something broadly similar within the confines of working online. It might be that you give the Samaritans' phone number, make suggestions for other avenues of support, or state what you are able to offer. If you are working with a client in a different country, you may not know what professional help is available in a crisis. You must offer only what you are sure you will able to supply. If you do not go online over the weekend, then it is useless to tell a client that, in a crisis, you will respond to an email out of office hours.

The contract then deals with confidentiality. What is written below applies in the UK and would obviously have to be changed to reflect other countries' laws and requirements for supervision. You might wish to include details of your supervisor, so that the client can contact them if there are problems between you. You would need to have your supervisor's agreement to do this. As we would hope that the client would discuss difficulties in our relationship or work with us first, we do not give that information in the contract, although we would be willing to give it if we could not resolve the issues between ourselves.

Confidentiality
The content of our work together is confidential, within these exceptions. The first is that all counsellors in the UK are in regular confidential supervision, where we discuss our work to ensure that we are working in the most effective way to enable our clients to reach their goals.

Secondly, if I believe that you are at risk, or putting others at risk, I might need to break confidentiality. Some UK laws in some circumstances require me to break confidentiality, such as the Terrorism Act, The Children Act, Proceeds of Crime and Road Traffic Act.

In most cases I would endeavour to notify you of this first, although there are occasionally legal reasons why this might not be possible.

The above paragraph does not deal with confidentiality in terms of security of emails sent and received by both you and the client. In Chapter 4, confidentiality, privacy, encryption and the use of a portable key drive are explored in detail. In a contract, we would mention this aspect, and send the client a prepared document that tells them how they can maintain privacy on their own computer, particularly stressing the fact that the use of workplace and public computers may mean that other people could access their emails to me.

At the most basic level, clients often forget that it may be possible for family or other people they share a computer with, or even who simply live in the same house, to access their mail, or stored Messenger sessions, if these are not password protected. Sometimes their password is known to others, perhaps because they use the same one for everything. While initially the client may feel that it would not matter if their partner/friend did happen to read a therapeutic email, they may later be writing things that they would not wish anyone else to read.

Another aspect of confidentiality and privacy is to draw the client's attention to the physical space in which they are writing to you, or 'talking' to you. If the computer is in a shared space it may mean, at best, that they can be interrupted, and, at worst, that someone can read over their shoulder what they are writing.

Having stressed the need to make clients aware, perhaps we also need to remind ourselves that, even in f2f work, walls are sometimes thin, and so a conversation may be overheard. The balance has to be struck between sensible and safe precautions and becoming over-anxious about confidentiality. In the end, we can point out some of the pitfalls, suggest suitable ways of protecting the work, and then we need to leave it up to the client.

The paragraph you might use here could run:

Privacy
My computer is password protected, is not used by anyone else, and is in my counselling room. To help you to decide how to ensure the privacy of emails you send and receive in our work together, I am attaching a separate Word document with some ideas. If anything is not clear, do ask me about this.

Because technology can and does fail at times, you should make arrangements ahead of problems, so that if they do happen, you both have a clear sense of the procedure. If you ensure that you can access your mail service from a web-based account, in practice you can send an email from a public internet point. This can be useful, for example, if you need to tell a client that your computer has crashed, although you may feel that you would not wish to send therapeutic emails from there.

Making sure that you have good IT back-up if necessary can help you feel more secure. You may be very IT literate and not need this, but knowing you can get helpful service from your internet provider, and/or having someone you can call on to resolve the problem speedily, be that a friend or a professional source, is essential for many of us.

A paragraph dealing with technology might read as follows:

Technology
Working online means that there are occasionally technological problems. If you are unable to get online, you may wish to leave me a telephone message on 01234 567890 or send a text message to my mobile phone 07234 567890. (These are UK codes – if you are outside the UK, you will need to use the international code for the UK.) You may want to give me a means of contacting you if I cannot get online.

If I do not hear from you that you have received my email within 72 hours of sending it, I will resend it, in case there has been a problem. If I then do not hear from you, I will assume that you do not wish to continue working with me. If at any point during our work together you decide that you wish to end our contract, I would very much appreciate it if you would let me know this.

AGREEMENT

You may feel that you have included everything in the contract, and that it is all quite clear. However, clients may misunderstand, particularly if they are anxious, or there may be something that you have not thought of, for which they need an answer. For that reason, it is sensible to invite them briefly to raise any points to which they might need answers. Thus:

> When you have read this contract, and clarified any points, please send the form below back to me by email. We can then begin to work therapeutically.
> I am looking forward to hearing back from you.

This also suggests that the work will not begin until the contract is agreed. The 'form below' refers to a statement that demonstrates their agreement to the terms of the contract, and may also include any background information you feel you need. The statement might read:

> I have read the contract for working with Anne Stokes, and agree to its terms.
> I would like to work by email / MSN (please tick your choice).
> I will pay by cheque / PayPal / bank transfer (please indicate your choice).
>
> Name ....
>
> Date ....

The personal information you require might include contact telephone number and address. You could choose to write 'optional' after these (or any other questions) as the client may want anonymity. The age might be important to you, as you might not want to work with people under a certain age. Is gender always obvious from the names clients use, or does this need to be asked? It may be useful to know if they are on any medication, working with other health professionals, alcohol consumption, use of any non-prescribed drugs, suicidal thoughts, or previous experience of counselling. Depending on your orientation, you may also want to ask them about family of origin and/or current family, or what their occupation is. Asking about what other support networks they have (e.g. friends, family, church etc.) may be useful for you, should there be a crisis. You can probably add other things that you would like to know.

All of these may be useful for you to know, so that you do not have to ask about them later, but it is also important to consider how the client may react. They may feel fine about giving information, and indeed expect a professional counsellor to ask such questions. On the other hand, it could make them shy away from engaging with you at this stage, as they feel they are being asked to disclose too much. Once again, it may depend on how you work face to face and how flexible you are prepared to be in this situation.

If you always use a form that asks a number of similar questions to those given above, then initially it may feel comfortable to adapt that for online use, and ask your clients to fill it in. You may later want to adapt it further in light of any feedback you receive, or the way in which questions are answered (or not!). If you never use an assessment tool, or an intake interview, asking any of these things may feel alien to you. Again, perhaps begin without asking them, then if you find that it is more difficult to pick up such information in online than in f2f work, you might want to devise something that gives you some background. There is no one right way of doing this, and of course, many things that we could verify face to face, are not apparent online. Your 21-year-old female client could in fact be an 84-year-old male!

In an international online case study discussion group on contracting, one participant stated that she does not ask for information because she sees that level of trust developing at a different pace online (Jones, 2002). Another stated that the biggest learning curve was to put a lid on all her questions, and to ask for information as and when it was necessary, such as 'are you taking any medication?'

To encourage you to think more about how *you* would want to write your contract, you might choose to undertake the activities below before reading the next chapters, which look at how you work therapeutically with clients.

Practice activities

1 Carry out a search to access the web pages of counsellors working online. Study their contracts, noting any style differences, national or state differences, and content. Draw up a list of points that you would also like to include in your own contract.

2 Devise a contract that you might use with online clients. Remember to write in a style that suits the way you work. Ask both a counsellor colleague and a friend to read it and comment on its clarity and user-friendliness. Revise it if necessary.

3 If you are already working online and have an established form of contract, review it in light of anything that has occurred to you as you read this chapter. Again, you might want to ask someone else to read it as well.

Chapter 4

Counselling Asynchronously by Email and Message Board

INTRODUCTION

This chapter explores asynchronous (time-delayed) counselling. Technology provides the means for people to communicate asynchronously by email or by writing messages in a specially designed passworded space on a website (known as a message board). The first part of this chapter demonstrates counselling asynchronously in practice. There are suggestions about organizing and structuring your time when working online as well as some examples of therapeutic responses. We also consider how to challenge asynchronously and how to deal with online silence from the client. In the second part we discuss some practical aspects of working online, including maintaining confidentiality, encryption, digital signatures and computer privacy. Some boundary issues that are relevant to both synchronous and asynchronous counselling are discussed in Chapter 10. We begin this chapter with a brief description of the two main methods of asynchronous counselling.

COUNSELLING BY EMAIL

Email counselling consists of email exchanges between counsellor and client (one email each way constitutes one email exchange). The therapeutic text may form the main body of the email or could be sent as a file attachment with a covering email. Any file can be attached to an email, so picture and sound files may also be used in online counselling (see Chapter 7 for more information).

COUNSELLING BY PRIVATE MESSAGE BOARD

In counselling by private message board both counsellor and client visit a password-protected area of a website to receive, read, store and send private messages to each other. Message boards can be accessed from any computer that is connected to the internet. This is particularly useful if the client shares a computer since all confidential material is stored behind a password and no one else can access it unless they know the web address and password. However, messages are not delivered to an email program (the recipient has to visit a website to collect messages) and unless there is a special arrangement (e.g. an email to alert the recipient) neither counsellor nor client knows when a message has been left for them.

COUNSELLING ASYNCHRONOUSLY IN PRACTICE

Before the therapeutic work begins, you may have exchanged two or three preliminary emails with your client agreeing the contract and outlining arrangements for how and when you will be in touch. The client will have told you a little about the issues they want to examine in counselling and you will have begun to build a relationship with them. Confidentiality and privacy will have been discussed, and you will have made an initial assessment of their suitability for online counselling (ISMHO). This part of the chapter will show you some examples of asynchronous counselling in practice and the word 'email' will be used to describe both emails and message boards.

Timing of counselling exchanges

The timing options for asynchronous counselling are a key element in setting up a therapeutic agreement. They will determine when both counsellor and client may expect to be in communication. It is important to check expectations and assumptions about when messages are received and answered as clear arrangements facilitate a supportive environment for both client and counsellor. The following example shows how some online counsellors clarify when they will be in contact.

> Emails can be exchanged in different ways in my online counselling service and I ask you to indicate your preference in the Client section of this Agreement.
> 1. You may want to write to me as often as you like, knowing I will respond to all your emails on a set day each week (e.g. Thursday).
> 2. You may want me to respond to each email as I receive it. I normally reply to emails within 48 hours and will let you know when this is not possible.
> 3. You may want to make a weekly payment to exchange as many emails with me as you choose during an agreed week.
> I call my main email response to you a Therapeutic Email (TE) and that is the one I charge for. (I number the emails in a pre-paid package in the subject line as TE1/3 or TE2/5 etc.) You may have a query after you have read a TE and I reply briefly to such queries at no additional charge. Any administrative emails (e.g. to query something I have written or to book a live session) are also not charged for.

Once the counselling agreement goes to the client, some online counsellors will also signal that the therapeutic work begins after it is completed and returned. How therapy begins will be a matter of personal choice. Some online counsellors may ask clients to complete forms giving life history and background details or complete questionnaires and mood inventories; others will ask clients to write about the issue that's bringing them to counselling. It is sometimes helpful to the client if the counsellor gives them a prompting question or phrase such as they might use with a new client in their counselling room. If their normal style is to sit and wait for the client to start when they are ready, this needs to be explained to the client in writing.

The length of client emails is also a matter of preference. Some online counsellors like to indicate what is an acceptable amount for a client to write in a single email. Others prefer to encourage them to write as much as they like because they find the additional material is useful therapeutically. Some counsellors will indicate what length of reply a client might expect from them no matter how long the client email is. Where clients write brief (less than 15 lines) emails it is helpful if the counsellor keeps their reply to a similar length as the client may have a physical or reading difficulty which they have not mentioned.

Organizing yourself

Keep a record of the number of email 'sessions' you hold with clients. Some counsellors do this by booking time in their diary for each email. Keeping a diary record allows them to see what point in therapy has been reached with any single client and whether or not they have room for a new client when they receive a new enquiry.

On our training courses we suggest that when replying to a client email, counsellors take the same measures as would take for an f2f client. They do not answer the phone or the doorbell, they shut the door to their office and work on the client email in privacy and without interruption; however, they can do the allotted online work at a time that is convenient to them, wear what they like and have a drink beside them while they work. There is a great temptation to respond to a client email the moment it is received. This is fine if you are confident about your understanding of what the client has written. Suler (1998) has a '24 hour Rule' that he adopts with emails about which he is uncertain. He writes his reply, then sets it on one side for 24 hours before re-reading and sending it, allowing time for adjustment if his understanding of the client changes. On our training courses we recommend that counsellors reply to their clients, then re-read both the client email and their reply before sending to make sure they still feel they have answered the client's issues with understanding. If they are uncertain, they are encouraged to wait 24 hours before re-reading and sending as an added safeguard.

Therapeutic email responses

Email responses can be laid out in various ways. Some counsellors like to keep the client's text and write their responses inside it (building a dialogue). Others prefer to reply using brief quotations from the client's email in their reply. Still others might write their reply as a Word document, using sophisticated formatting (e.g. bullet point lists, coloured fonts, images, poems, etc.) and attach it to a covering email – like putting a letter inside an envelope.

Whether you choose dialogue, separate file attachment or single email is a mixture of personal preference and the complexity of the client's issues. Single emails work well with clients who are focusing on a single issue; the dialogue style is helpful when the client's email ranges over different issues and you can respond to each. A formatted reply picks out important points in the text and is particularly helpful if your client has reading difficulties.

Single emails

Some counsellors respond with a single email in their own words with perhaps some quotations from the client email. For example:

> Hello H, I am sitting at my computer ready to give your email my undivided attention. After reading it, I felt angry and helpless (*H sounds alone and isolated here, it seems as though everything she tries, fails, and people seem to be turning away rather than helping her*). Does that describe what life is like for you at the moment? Please let me know if I've misunderstood something in your next email. If I'm right you probably found it very painful writing these thoughts down and perhaps we've only touched the tip of the iceberg(?). Let's see if I can summarize what I think are the most important features of what you have written so far. I'll begin with a quotation which really shot off the page at me: 'I don't believe I've ever been really happy since my Nan died.' *<Feeling sad as I read this>* You sound very sad here and maybe it was a really important statement to make and painful to write(?) Perhaps you will want to say some more about it in your next email . . .

In the example above, the counsellor has marked out the client quotation using both quotation marks and the client's font choice. If the email doesn't allow for different fonts, the counsellor could have emboldened the client's words or underlined them as an alternative way of distinguishing them from the counsellor's own text.

Repeating the client's words back to them both validates what they wrote and signifies the importance the counsellor attaches to them. They have also added their personal response to the writing using italics and angle brackets < > to denote that these are asides from the main text of the email, and put question marks in brackets to show they are tentative about what they have written.

Dialogue emails

Responding within the client's text is a useful way of dealing with a long client email which may touch on many issues. This style splits the text into manageable amounts and takes one point at a time. Counsellors who work in this way are responding to all the different thoughts that the client is bringing and are thus less likely to miss something. Kraus *et al.* (2004) discuss the usefulness for the client of re-reading their own words with the counsellor's thoughts beside them, so the thoughts become 'a reflection of his or her own inner wisdom' (p. 168). The dialogue style means that clients read their own words again. The two 'voices' are sometimes shown by different coloured fonts but these (as mentioned above) may not show up if the client's email program is set to Plain Text. If this is the case, you can write your reply as a Word document using colours to show the different voices and send this as a file attachment with a covering email. A typical dialogue might look something like this (the client's words are in their own font and the counsellor has put quotation marks around them, too).

> 'I've noticed a shift in the way I am with my mum, particularly when we argue. I now see she's just like the rest of us, she has strengths and weaknesses and I've probably inherited a bit of each! We had another argument last week – over something as simple as travel directions. Previously I'd have brought up a lot of past arguments and made sure I had the last word so I could 'win' but this time I didn't. I just let it go – she had the last word and it felt OK. In fact I felt better for "allowing" her to have the last word as though I was more mature than she was! It felt good as well as a bit strange.'
>
> *How good it was to read this part of your email. I guess your mum will feel relieved not to have the past dragged up every time there is a disagreement <smiling here>. I can see that 'letting go of the past' is beginning to work for you and it's your determination and effort that's making this happen.*

The disadvantage of this style is the amount of reading involved as the dialogue grows, and the difficulty of distinguishing new text from old text if the dialogue continues through more than one counselling exchange. If the counselling is conducted in this way, it is more manageable if both counsellor and client take joint responsibility for removing text that is no longer relevant. When some of the dialogue belongs to previous emails, it is helpful to keep different font styles for the two voices but define the words that are 'old' (i.e. belong to previous email exchanges). In the example below, square brackets have been added to help distinguish old and new, and the counsellor's (GJ) words are in italics with their initials. The client's most recent words are put inside quotation marks and also have their initials (DS).

> [DS: I don't know where to begin really, I'm worried about my marriage, my children, my mother. I just seem to have stopped thinking again – like before. It feels like every part of my life is collapsing at the moment and I don't know what I can do to stop it. I just hope you can help me sort myself out. It's all such a muddle. **GJ: *From what I sense in your writing, you are concerned about different parts of your life and you don't know where to turn first(?) Do you think it might help if you try and focus on just one thing in your reply? I'm also aware that you feel you are reacting just like you have in the past and at this point I'm thinking to myself* <It sounds as though F's not giving any thought to caring for herself again and she could be the most important person to keep physically and mentally healthy in this household.> *I really want to say 'slow down, take a deep breath' let's talk through things one at a time.*]**

> 'DS: I have been thinking a lot since your last email. I agree with what you say about taking one thing at a time. So I've decided to put the latest crisis on one side until I feel stronger, then I can deal with it better. Worrying about everything doesn't work – I really need to concentrate on one thing at a time.' **GJ: *Thinking aloud here* <what a huge change F is making>. *Even though you're in a crisis right now, you're not 'frozen' by it this time. You're thinking things through more objectively.* <smiling to myself here> *This is a big step forward and a much more manageable way to look at things.***

Structuring the therapeutic response

When responding therapeutically to emails it is helpful to have some idea of structure. Students on our courses have found that a three-part structure similar to Egan's (1994) model for counselling of Exploration,

Understanding, Action works well when it is used as a background structure for emails. Some theoretical orientations will only use the first two stages of this model.

1 *Exploration* – the counsellor's understanding of the content of the client's email. It is often put as a brief summary of the theme(s) with suggestions of possible feelings put tentatively inside bracketed questionmarks and the counsellor's own feelings put inside angle brackets. Clients have found a summary validates their writing and offers an early opportunity to correct misunderstandings.
2 *Understanding* – the counsellor's empathic understanding not only of the content but of the deeper issues and feelings the client is not putting directly into words. It is also a chance for the counsellor to suggest wider perspectives and opportunities for re-framing. Tentative questionmarks in brackets are used here. Whatever therapeutic approach is used, understanding helps the client to feel heard and understood and any misunderstandings can be corrected.
3 *Action* – this will usually include suggestions about how to move the therapy forward, which may involve tasks and ideas for the client to think about or complete as homework.

As well as shaping the email content using the model above, online counsellors also include their personal responses to the client's email. Murphy and Mitchell (1998) suggest that these responses should be put in brackets as asides to the main text. Personal responses are a key part of this style of counselling. They show the client how the counsellor is feeling or indicate how they arrived at a particular understanding. Some clients will pick up on this and add their personal responses in asides as well, which strengthens and deepens both understanding and the working alliance. A typical response to a client using this framework might be as follows:

> Hi M, I'm ready to work on your email and after reading it through I'm feeling indignant and upset <*guess that might be how you felt(?)*>. I think just one sentence sums up for me what I understood from your email (correct me if I've got it wrong). 'M feels she is unimportant and misunderstood by people who are important to her.' It felt as though you were being dismissed as unimportant (*is that right?*) when your partner ignored what you said. You also wrote how your boss misheard what

you were saying to him yesterday and when you tried to correct him, he also ignored you. Now I'm sitting here wondering what it must be like to be misunderstood and ignored by the people who are important to you *<thinking aloud – it could be lonely when other people don't understand you or ignore you>*. I hope I've got this theme right – please let me know if it feels wrong. I was sitting here feeling angry for you when I read your email, I wanted you to tell them how you were feeling. But you kept 'quiet' and pretended 'not to care' so I'm wondering what you might have said had you not kept quiet. I think it might be helpful to explore your inner thoughts because I'm concerned you might be ignoring your feelings when you pretend 'not to care'. This could be one reason for the lack of confidence and insecurity you talked about in your first email to me.

   Hope this email is useful. I look forward to hearing more from you when you are ready,

   Warm regards,

   Gill Jones

Working by email, where neither client nor counsellor have visual (apart from the text), oral or aural information about the other, it is important to create a safe enough space for the working alliance to flourish and the counselling work to be done. We believe this is best achieved by creating the Rogerian core conditions of genuineness (congruence), empathy and unconditional positive regard. Online counsellors will find themselves using the basic skills they learned in their f2f training to create a suitable space for a working alliance. Unlike f2f clients, online clients are receiving their therapy at their own computers, often with the significant other about whom they have negative feelings uncomfortably close by.

Challenging online

Challenging the client therapeutically online needs to be handled with care if the client is not to walk away feeling criticized and misunderstood. For example, a mythical client presents with a series of failed relationships and no insight into their part in the failure. As this becomes clear to the counsellor, they want to challenge it without any further preparation so in their next email they write:

> I wonder if you've given any thought to the part you could have played in these failed relationships?

In an f2f setting these words could be said gently by the counsellor, perhaps with a smile; but written down, the words seem terse and brusque. Left like this, the counselling relationship could break down because the client feels misunderstood and judged by the counsellor. It is easier to walk away from an online counselling relationship than it is from one that is face to face. A more productive method would be to prepare the client for the challenge and offer them space to discuss their feelings about it.

> A question has been in my head for a while now and I think it's the right time to ask it. This question may make you feel angry at first but anger can block other feelings which could be helpful if we can identify them. The question is this. I wonder if you've given any thought to the part you could have played in these failed relationships? I look forward to discussing this further in your next email.

By preparing the client for the challenge and asking them to comment on how the question itself makes them feel rather than answering it directly should bring a more successful result.

Working with online silence

Unexpected breaks in the pattern of communication online can mean several different things. Sometimes there is a computer or other technology failure which has prevented normal contact, and many online counsellors will have made a prior agreement for such events. A typical arrangement might be to leave a text message on the other person's mobile phone, letting them know there is a technology emergency. There could also be a number of other reasons for an email silence from an online client, including:

- illness
- changes at work
- difficulties with a significant relationship
- some unforeseen life event (e.g. death of a family member)

- wanting to leave counselling for the time being because they find they have done sufficient work and want to put their learning into practice
- not finding therapy valuable or useful
- finding therapy too painful to continue.

When counsellors don't receive any email or information from the client, some will send an unsolicited email to check the position. For some counsellors any unsolicited contact by them interferes with their theoretical orientation, and some ethical practice codes might view such contact as interfering with the client's autonomy.

If an online counsellor wants to use this type of contact when a client has failed to communicate, the circumstances under which they will do so needs to be specified and agreed with the client at the contracting stage. Unsolicited emails need to be worded carefully if they are not to put the client under additional pressure to respond or feel guilty.

Here is a possible wording for this type of unsolicited email:

> Hello J, I hope all is well and you received my email which I sent three weeks ago. I thought I should write to let you know I haven't received any reply from you, just in case an email has gone astray. If you haven't had time to respond yet, please don't feel guilty and rush to respond to this email, but if you have responded, please could you re-send because it hasn't reached me. I look forward to further work with you when you are ready.
> Warm regards,
> Gill Jones

If the counsellor's reminder email is timely and worded appropriately it may lead to a deepening of the therapeutic relationship and further useful work.

PRACTICAL ASPECTS OF WORKING ASYNCHRONOUSLY ONLINE

There are many advantages to working online, which have been mentioned in earlier chapters. One of the main advantages of counselling asynchronously online is its convenience. Clients do not have to make arrangements to keep an appointment. It is suitable for those who would otherwise have to travel long distances to the counsellor's office, or who

---

Practice activities

Write a dialogue style of email reply to this client.

I've got in touch now because I need help with my present relationship. I'm very insecure and have never felt able to trust anybody, especially men.

I've been with my partner for a year now and I know I love him. he's very kind and deep down I know there's no reason not to trust him but if he even smiles at another female I feel panicky and jealous. Then I make some silly comment about them hoping he'll tell me I'm wrong and he only loves me but he gets angry and says I wouldn't say such things if I really loved him – so he blames me and then we argue even more.

I've been jealous in every relationship I've had and I really want to deal with it now, otherwise I'll lose him. I don't want that to happen, I want to enjoy life again.

I hope you can help me. D

---

would need to make complex arrangements for the care of others. It allows people with communication problems to receive help without involving third parties. Working asynchronously also means that both client and counsellor can work when they are ready and, unlike an f2f session, everything that is discussed can be stored on the computer and read again. Both client and counsellor have time to put together their thoughts without feeling under pressure to share them immediately; text can be changed and adjusted. This is helpful to the counsellor who is composing a considered reply, but excessive editing by the client can dilute or distort their feelings and some online counsellors encourage their clients to send emails just as they write them, without any re-reading or editing.

Once they have sent their email, clients feel they have shared their burden and can wait for their counsellor's response. This may be more substantial than they would hear in an f2f session and may take them time to understand. However, because the counsellor's words are written, clients can return to the email and read it over again and again. If the meaning is not clear or the client disagrees with the counsellor's understanding, they can correct this. Correcting each other acknowledges the potential for misunderstanding in the written word (discussed in Chapter 2) and promotes a collegial relationship which may not be possible in f2f work.

Asynchronous online counselling is also more discreet than live session or internet telephone. By choosing when to do the writing, clients can ensure that they are not interrupted and do not draw attention to themselves by their failure to attend an appointment.

There are also some disadvantages to counselling in this way. Besides the potential for misunderstanding the written word (mentioned above), a major disadvantage can be the nature of asynchronous communication. Recipients do not receive a reply instantly and may be left wondering for some days if their email has been received. To ease this uncertainty some online counsellors will suggest each of them attach a 'read receipt' (sometimes called a 'return receipt') to their email for confirmation of its delivery, although 'read receipts' do not work with all email programs. Some counsellors will send a holding reply on receipt of a client email, saying the client email has been received and when they can expect a response.

The time lapse between writing and responding also means that the counsellor is responding to an email which the client has written in the past (even if this is only a few minutes ago). There is no way of knowing if the client will be in the same situation by the time they read the counsellor's reply. Fenichel (2007) says 'in between the expression of an intense feeling or concern, and the response to it, there may be [some] intervening events or thoughts which the therapist needs to be aware of as well, particularly if there has been a time delay'. One way of dealing with time lapse is to refer to the client's feelings using the past tense and allowing for the possibility of changes in the intervening time. Here's an example.

> In your email you described some very powerful thoughts and feelings when you spotted Y in the distance. I'm wondering how you feel about her now and whether you think you'd have the same reaction if you saw her again?

Confidentiality and privacy

Confidentiality poses a challenge for asynchronous counselling, even when the client is meticulous about not leaving an email or message open on the computer screen. An email can be read by anyone who happens to intercept it while it is waiting on a web server (see Glossary) to be collected by the recipient's email program. In fact, where any kind of workplace network or intranet is involved, confidentiality can be compromised as IT technicians have access to anything that is held on the local server waiting to be collected. Emails can also be read by anyone else who has access to the client's email inbox – this would include anyone who knows the password (if they have a shared email inbox) or an employer, if the client is using a company computer.

Encryption and Digital Signatures

One solution to the problem of confidentiality is to encrypt the emails and messages. US Practitioner Codes (see Appendix) recommend that all counselling emails are encrypted and many encryption programs are very effective when used by both counsellor and client. Two programs that offer a free version of their software (hushmail and safe-mail) change the email's text into a complex code which can only be understood when decrypted. Emails can be stored, sent and received at the encryption website. Some versions of encryption programs (which need a bit of computer confidence to set up) embed their encryption software inside an email program so that the user can access all their emails from one place. Another security feature is digital signing of emails, which verifies that the email has indeed been sent by the originator and has not been changed in transit (most encryption programs also digitally sign their encrypted emails). Some online counsellors think digital signatures are unnecessary as they say their clients recognize that the email has come from them by their written style and choice of language but it could be prudent to use a digital signature at the beginning of a counselling contract.

Computer Privacy

However, no amount of encryption or digital signatures will protect emails that are sent, received and stored (decrypted) on a computer. Online counsellors may need to show clients how to keep their counselling emails private. Before you can do this you should know how to keep your own work private and your computer secure. Here are some questions for you to ask yourself about where and how you will keep transcripts and notes about online client work.

- Are client emails kept on a computer to which only you have access? If not, where and how will you store transcripts and notes of online client work? (On a key drive? CD? floppy disk? external drive?)

■ Does your computer ask for a password or fingerprint identity every time you open it from both Start Up and Screensaver positions? (Is your computer secure enough for confidential work?)

■ Once the work has ended, how long and where will you store the online counselling transcripts and notes? (Storage of counselling work is discussed in Chapter 11.)

If you do not have answers to these questions, you should give some thought to them before engaging in confidential work with clients.

Once you are clear about your own levels of protection for client work, you may want to discuss levels of privacy with your online clients and discover whether this is an issue for them or not. In particular, you might want to check if the client shares their computer either at home or at work. Where a computer is shared, the simplest and cheapest solution might be to suggest that they acquire a new email address with a remote web server such as Hotmail or Yahoo and keep their password private. Emails can be read, sent and stored at the website, and curious strangers who might be checking through the computer's history and temporary internet files (to see which websites have been visited) will be asked to log in with a user name and password if they try to access the contents of a mailbox. One drawback to this might be if a client's 'significant other' becomes suspicious of the regular visits to Hotmail or Yahoo. If this is the case, the client may need to know how to delete their cyber 'footprint' from these places every time they visit the website; you may need to know how to do this in order to help a client. (This involves finding and deleting the computer's memory cache of temporary internet files and browser history pages.)

Using a portable USB, Mobile or Key Drive

One way to keep emails confidential and computer history files 'clean' is to use a portable storage drive (variously known as a portable key drive, USB drive or mobile drive), which plugs into a USB port on any computer. A client downloads a mobile version of their web browser (e.g. Internet Explorer) on to the USB drive and opens an email account with, say, Hotmail. When they want to collect emails or read them, they plug the USB drive into a computer connected to the internet and open the *mobile* web browser to visit their email account. They read and respond to their emails and, when they have finished, they close everything down and remove the key drive. There is no cyber 'footprint' in the computer's history or temporary internet files (that's all on the USB drive). The computer only registers that a USB port has been opened and closed. The client will, of course, need a secure place to store their USB drive (many of them fit on to key rings) and some of them can be password protected for extra security.

CONCLUSION

This chapter has looked at how asynchronous counselling takes place, and the advantages and disadvantages of this type of counselling. We have discussed management of time and personal space for asynchronous online counsellors, and considered how therapeutic emails or messages might be laid out, the different ways of styling responses and how to challenge or manage silence online. In the next chapter we examine how online counselling works in synchronous sessions in a private chatroom.

Suggestions for asynchronous counselling

1 Check client's views on confidentiality/privacy before beginning the work (educate where necessary).
2 Organize your time to focus on a client email efficiently.
3 Contract timing of emails, management of silences and ways of signalling that messages have been sent/received.
4 Shape your responses using a model such as Exploration, Understanding, Action.
5 Allow for misunderstanding in your replies.
6 Put your personal responses (thoughts/feelings) as asides using <> or () to deepen the relationship.
7 Match shorter emails (to allow for possible unidentified reading disability).
8 Demonstrate core conditions of genuineness (congruence), empathy and unconditional positive regard in words to build a relationship and compensate for missing visual/aural/oral cues.
9 If formatting is necessary (e.g. bulleted lists, coloured fonts, image, sound, charts and forms), send as email file attachments.
10 Before sending, re-read both client and counsellor emails to check for understanding.

Chapter 5

Counselling Synchronously by Live Chat-room Session

In the previous chapters we have mainly concentrated on online counselling via email. However, sessions in 'real time' using 'chat rooms' (for example, Messenger or counsellors' own designated chat rooms) are an alternative. Perhaps at this stage it is important to underline again that we do not see one form of online counselling as better or worse. The choice of which to use, or indeed a mixture of both, needs to be made in light of what works best for a particular counsellor and his or her clients. In this chapter, the pros and cons of the different methods of counselling will be made clear, before introducing how real-time work might be undertaken. Sometimes follow-up emails and/or evaluation of live sessions may be useful, as well as evaluation at the end of therapy, and these will be discussed.

INTERNET RELAY CHAT

If you are already familiar with talking to friends in real time, you may want to skip over this section, and move straight on to Using IRC for Counselling, on page 57. Internet relay chat (IRC) is a way of holding a live 'conversation' on the screen, using the computer's internet connection, with another person (or more than one person), who is online at the same time in a different location. Participants type in whatever they want to say, and this appears on the screens of both the sender and the receiver. Thus 'chat' is a medium for counselling online which offers a fast synchronous way of 'speaking' without any facial expressions, tone, or body language. It is possible to compensate for some of these 'missing elements' by using emotional bracketing and emoticons, and these will be discussed later in the chapter. In her research, Kasket (2003) suggests that, for some counsellors, using chat with clients feels like meeting together in a cyberspace location. Maybe this can help to create the 'safety of the counselling room' which is often associated with f2f therapy.

To set up this way of working, counsellor and client obviously both need access to the internet, and a chat room that is private and secure. Counsellors may set up their own chat/conference rooms on their websites, or, rather more easily for many people, join a service such as Messenger, for example through Hotmail. This is a free service, enabling you to 'talk' to your contacts any time when you and they are online at the same time in a private space. It can only be accessed by one participant inviting another into the 'room'. No one else can intrude on your conversation by mistake. The service itself is password protected, so that you can be sure that no one else reads your work with clients. It is worth reminding clients to choose a password that someone with whom they might share a computer will not be able to guess.

You can have any number of contacts, and these will be listed, with a symbol showing whether they are online or not. Anyone who is online is available for a 'conversation'. You contact someone by clicking on his or her name, and then clicking on the appropriate one of the messages that will appear – for example 'Send an instant message' or 'Send an email'. In the box below, you will see six contact names listed. Frank's name has been clicked on, and various possibilities appear beside his name. If you wanted to start a Messenger conversation with him, you would click on 'Send an instant message'.

Frank	Send an instant message
	Send email
	Call
	Video
	View
	Edit contact
	Block contact
	Delete contact
Gill	
Jo	
Lizzie	
Lucy	
Mike	

Once you have clicked on the instant message facility, a screen will appear which shows your message and any that the person you have contacted types in return. Examples of this will be given later.

Using Messenger does not mean that your client may talk to you whenever they feel like it, simply because they see you are online! Part of your contracting will have been around the times of appointments, making it clear that at other times you are not available to talk. Some counsellors have an agreement that if they are online and the client is in crisis, contact is possible. In that case, it is up to the counsellor to keep the strict boundaries of crisis contact in place and ensure that they are not abused.

However, for day-to-day use of Messenger, you can use a series of options to show your online status. For example, you can use 'Appear offline', which will show you as offline on your contacts' screens, even though you are still connected to the internet and can do all your other normal tasks there, such as reading and sending emails, and searching the web. Other signs you can use are 'Away', 'Busy' or 'Out to lunch'. If you are using your own conference room from your website, these precautions are less necessary, as you will not access it unless you have a prearranged appointment.

One advantage of a chat room such as Messenger over a dedicated chat/conference room is that many of the latter may not be sufficiently sophisticated to show when someone is typing. Messenger has a message at the base of the screen that reads 'Anne is typing a message' when Anne is typing. Knowing that the other person is writing prevents you 'speaking' over each other. It also makes it easier to tolerate a pause or a silence if you know that your client is writing. Even if no words are appearing on your screen, you can see that every so often they are writing something. If what eventually arrives on your screen is no more than a few words, you have some sense of the struggle they have had to say whatever it is. If appropriate, you can comment on this. 'It feels as if it was very hard for you to tell me that' or 'I'm wondering if it was difficult to find the words just now.'

Without this indication of what is happening on the client's computer, you have no idea whether they are still there, are waiting for you to say something or whether there is some other explanation. If that happens, you will need to decide whether it is therapeutically right to break the silence, or hold it. Without body language to convey the meaning in the silence, it might be better to risk breaking the silence than have your client experience it as punishing or withholding.

An example of a group meeting between several people in a training session is shown below, although in practice unless you intend to work with groups, only you and the client will be in the conversation. Later in the chapter, we look at how users can help distinguish between participants quickly in a conversation.

> Penny says:
> Are we all ready to make a start as it's 2.00 pm?
> Mary says:
> Yep
> **Hilary says:**
> **yes**
> Anne says:
> yes
> Penny says:
> Hi Hilary, I'm glad you managed to make it.

USING IRC FOR COUNSELLING

Some clients may already be familiar with chat rooms and talking to friends in this way, while for others this will be a new experience, and the counsellor may have to help them become familiar with using synchronous communication. It is therefore important that the counsellor ascertain the client's previous experience before beginning the contract. Anthony (2003) notes that working in chat rooms brings different challenges from working through email communication, and this applies to both the client and the counsellor.

When you are working this way, you will need to take account of individual clients' rhythm as they write. This enables you to know the speed at which they usually write, judge what is a comfortable silence or pause and what is not, and also how they usually structure their writing (formally or informally, for example). Taking note of this will help you watch out for differences that may mean a different mood, a desire to say less or more, or that the client is struggling with a difficult issue. This is similar to noting changes in speech or tone when working face to face.

You will also need to be comfortable and reasonably fluent in using the written word as a means of communication. It may also help if you can write concisely in responding. If you normally tend to be voluble in spoken conversations, you may have to practise brevity online without losing meaning or empathy. You may also have to discover whether the client has good enough communication skills using live chat, or whether it puts them under extra pressure.

In some ways, the counsellor has to be more alert than in email counselling. There may be pauses as the client writes, particularly if they are writing a number of sentences at once. It can be easy to 'tune out' and think about other things while a client is responding, which could mean that you do not take in fully what is being said. In the same way, be aware that the client may be doing exactly the same at the other end, and have been distracted by something in their environment.

Although unlike email counselling, the counsellor has to be able to respond more instantly, without having much time to reflect on what has been written, there is slightly more time perhaps than in f2f work as you read the client's words. This is particularly so if they have been 'sent' in a series of short messages.

> Client says:
> I have been thinking about my relationship with my mother again . . .
> Client says:
> And I think I'd like to spend a bit of time looking at that today . . .
> Client says:
> It is hard to get her to accept that I am now 30 and leading an independent life. Probably because I stayed at home after my father died,

and went to a university in the next town, so lived at home . . .
Client says:
she still sees me as her child and not as an adult. Since I moved out a
few months ago, she has really tried to interfere with my life, and insist
on being still a part of it . . .
Client says:
That sounds a bit nasty of me, as I know she means well.

In this fictitious extract, the client has pressed 'send' after each time she
has typed a short message and so her words have appeared on the counsellor's screen in batches. This gives some space for the counsellor to think
about what is being said, rather more than there would be in f2f work as
it takes longer to type and send the words than to speak them.

Counselling using synchronous communication is suitable with both
long- and short-term clients. Unlike f2f work, it can be continuous even if
counsellors are away from home, provided that they have their laptop
with them, and internet access. However, don't be tempted to use an internet café for this purpose as you cannot ensure confidentiality, and working
in a public place does not feel very respectful of the client.

Finally, if you are using Messenger, you can choose to have a picture
beside your name, which will appear beside the screen when you are
'talking' to someone. You can also have a message that is shown alongside
your name on other people's contact lists. If you are using Messenger for
contacting both clients and friends or family, think carefully about photos,
other pictures, or written messages. Do you want a picture of you with
your children or cat to appear on clients' screens? Or the message, 'Away
with the fairies' (a niece's favourite!) beside your name? These are entirely
suitable for friends and family but may be rather less suitable for clients.
It sounds obvious, but if you have been contacting people online for years,
you may not think of this when setting up synchronous counselling
sessions.

ADVANTAGES OF SYNCHRONOUS COUNSELLING

One of the practical advantages of synchronous sessions is that it allows
the counsellor and the client to plan their work more easily than with
email exchanges. Times are agreed and put into diaries. This can be done
at the beginning of a contract (e.g. 'we will meet on each Thursday

between 9 and 10 a.m. UK time') or the next session can be arranged at the end of each live session to accommodate the client's diary. The latter is useful if they do not have a fixed work or home structure that would enable times to be settled ahead for a number of sessions. This is very similar to working face to face; some counsellors choose to have only fixed regular sessions, while others can, or indeed prefer, to do the opposite and have a degree of flexibility within scheduled appointments. It may depend also on the theoretical approach of the counsellor as to which option will be offered to the client (see also Chapter 9).

Sometimes working online is a second choice for a client, who might have preferred f2f counselling – for example someone who cannot locate a counsellor in their area, or has a difficulty in leaving their home. In that case, working in real time may provide them with a better sense of 'meeting' their counsellor. Whether it is actually the case or not, some clients feel that they get to know their counsellor more in this medium, have a stronger impression of their presence, and judge that they are able to form a 'real' relationship. The counsellor may also hold that perspective, and whether this is an advantage or a disadvantage will again depend on your own model of counselling.

When the counselling session is held in real time, there may be more spontaneity, with the client writing things that they would have edited out or refined if they had been engaged in email counselling. This can help to give the counsellor greater insight into what is actually going on for the client. Thus there is the opportunity for clarifying the meaning of the client's words or sorting out misunderstandings at the time, which may help to prevent issues from arising further down the line.

Marty says:
We have now made the decision not to have a child, which I am pleased about. And I want to sort out my career plans too.
Anne says:
Marty, just before looking at your career plans, could I just check out something about your decision?
Marty says:
Sure.
Anne says:
I'm not sure whether you meant that you were pleased that you'd decided against having a child, or whether you meant that you were

pleased to have got a decision made. I know being in limbo around the decision has been difficult for you, so I wanted to check which you meant. Hope that's OK to ask.

If you are in doubt about meaning, you will need to be able to convey that through the written word in a manner that does not leave the client feeling that they have 'got it wrong' or shamed that they have not been clear. On the other hand, it could be argued that when we speak or write in real time, we do not always say clearly what we mean, so the counsellor has to beware of taking it as 'the truth' simply because it has emerged raw, or apparently unedited.

An advantage over f2f sessions (unless taped), which is also shared with email counselling, is that there is a record of the conversation. This is done automatically on the latest versions of Messenger, so that there is a 'history' of all conversations with that contact, and can be done manually if using a designated conference room without this facility. To do this, simply open a Word document, highlight all the text, then copy and paste it into the document. Because it is not automatically saving as you go in the latter instance, it can be helpful if you do this periodically during the session. This prevents text being lost if the internet connection fails. However, if you find it distracting to do this during a session, you may choose not to do it, and hope that technology does not fail.

It makes good ethical sense to inform clients if you are saving the session, and to offer to send them a copy of the transcript. If it is being saved automatically for them, remind them of this, both so they know that they can re-access it, and so that they are aware of the need to make sure that they have thought about privacy and confidentiality.

Having the transcript allows both parties to go back and reflect on the session if they wish to do so, and for the counsellor, it can be very helpful to have this for supervision purposes. On the other hand, a supervisor reading part of a transcript sometimes may not gain insight into the climate of the session. It may seem strange to suggest that a counsellor knows when there is a sense of excitement or fear when they only have the written word to go on. However, when used to working this way, many counsellors can pinpoint changes in atmosphere during an exchange. This may be based on a difference in the speed of the exchanges, for example. Obviously, a supervisor does not have any insight into this.

DISADVANTAGES OF SYNCHRONOUS COUNSELLING

Chapter 4 stated that one of the main advantages of counselling asynchronously is its convenience, with clients not having to make arrangements to keep an appointment. However, the opposite is obviously true for synchronous work. This may simply be a preference, or reflect life styles and structures. Finding an hour to arrange to 'talk' online might be difficult to schedule, or the client may prefer to have more time to be able to reflect on what the counsellor has written.

Another disadvantage is a lack of confidentiality and privacy, an issue dealt with in more detail below. In spite of precautions, clients may still be interrupted, or their shared or workplace computer may allow access by others and, depending who reads what is on their computer, this may be an issue. For example, under normal circumstances a client might 'chat' to friends while sitting with their partner, or use the same password to sign in to their shared computer, so that both have free access to each other's stored history of online conversations. However, if talking to their counsellor, they may not wish to be in the same room, or may not want their partner to be able to read these conversations at a later date.

The typing ability and speed of both client and counsellor could be an issue. If either of you type very slowly, then the conversation can become protracted and not flow easily. Initially, both of you may find that you are taking care to type correctly, concentrating on spelling and punctuation, rather than on the meaning you are trying to convey. This tends to happen more in the early stages of working synchronously, but can be stultifying. As the counsellor becomes more used to working with clients in real time, they usually relax, and this seems to enable the client to relax as well. It perhaps parallels f2f work when newly trained counsellors, as well as those who are more experienced but meeting a new client, pick their words very carefully, but then relax as the relationship builds and they feel more settled or comfortable.

When working by email contact, as has been said previously both counsellor and client have more time to reflect before replying. In the main, this is likely to be a disadvantage of synchronous therapy. However, it could also be the opposite. Kasket (2003) observed that one of the participants in her research project commented that the luxury of time to reflect also might lead to going off on a tangent. Over-analysing the content of a client's email could risk moving away from the essence of the communication, or concentrating on what the counsellor can 'do' for the client rather than on staying with being with the client.

WORKING WITH CLIENTS SYNCHRONOUSLY

Before beginning work in real time with a client, a counsellor needs to pay as much attention to contracting as when working by email. There will be some additional features to the contract to ensure that privacy and confidentiality in this medium are as secure as possible. In addressing this, you may wish to spell certain things out. For example, Munro (2007) states on her website that the counselling can take place in the private chat room on her site, or that, if clients prefer, an encrypted chat room can be used. She clearly points out that in the latter case copies cannot be made of the session.

As well as commenting on the need for clients to ensure auditory and physical privacy to enable self-disclosure and guarantee confidentiality, Sampson *et al.* (1997) suggest that counsellors should monitor client behaviour during sessions and, if they believe that privacy has been compromised, they should take steps to remedy the situation. For example, this could be done by checking out the situation, and if necessary suggesting that it is terminated and a new appointment set up.

Counsellors also need to be aware of 'nettiquette', which is the generally used term for the unofficial rules and language that should be followed to keep within an acceptable way of communicating. As more and more people use text messaging through telephones and also online, some of these 'rules' become stretched to the very limits of polite conversation, so counsellors need to stay well within the boundaries when talking with clients, and avoid anything that might be construed as dubious, even if the client does not do this.

Some of the basic nettiquette rules to remember:

- Keep to the same standards that you would use with f2f clients
- Using capitals suggests that you are SHOUTING
- If your responses are full of errors, it may suggest you do not care about them
- Respect time boundaries, so you do not abuse clients' time
- Check whether the client likes or dislikes the use of emoticons
- If you use abbreviations, make sure your client has understood them
- Don't pretend you have understood an abbreviation if you haven't
- Think about the font and colour of text you are using – what might they suggest about you to a client?

In the above list, emoticons and abbreviations have been mentioned. These are explained below.

Emoticons are either clusters of punctuation to represent emotions, or 'smileys' that a service such as Messenger has as part of its instant messaging package. They are used to suggest the tone in which the previous phrase or sentence has been delivered, or as a response to something that has been said.

Some of the most widely used and understood punctuation marks are:

:-D laughing
;)   winking
:-O surprise
:(sad
:)   smile
8-} worried frown
>:(angry
:-/ scowling
:'-(crying

Although some emoticons can be created from the keyboard strokes such as 😊 by typing : plus) or 😞 by typing : plus (, most will be used directly from those provided by Messenger. Some examples of emoticons are shown below.

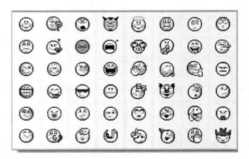

There are some that will provide movement on the screen. For example, there is a dancing *Lol!*, which is an exclamation mark that bounces on the page. Be very wary of using these until you know your client. They may be lovely and amusing to you, but your client may find them too flippant, or it may cause the conversation to become too much like a chat with a friend, and not a therapy session.

Another cautionary note here: once you have copied and saved a new emoticon into your storage space on Messenger (investigate the Messenger program for instructions), you may find that it takes on a life of its own. For example, a picture of a cat that someone in the conversation was using was copied and saved, as it seemed rather beautiful. Later, it was discovered that, in an online conversation, every time a word was written that had the letters c a t in them, in that order (communi**cat**e, **cat**ering, alter-**cat**ion, for example), this wretched cat would automatically appear instead of those three letters in the word!

The use of emoticons can be extremely useful as long as your clients are not unsettled by their appearance, or use them themselves. They can demonstrate empathy, or express a feeling succinctly. If in doubt about their value, ask your client, and be guided by their response.

Abbreviations are also a way of shortcutting the need to type out every word. As with emoticons, over-use of abbreviations can detract from the counselling process, be likened to texting a friend, and be thoroughly confusing. You could spend a lot of time trying to work out what **IYSWIM** meant (If you see what I mean). This could be distracting from what is going on and distancing if you felt excluded by someone who appeared to be in the know. Of course, once you have the sense and courage to ask, all is revealed. Some clients may not wish to tell you that they do not know what you mean. On the other hand, if your client is a regular texter, they may well use many abbreviations that you do not understand and you may need to say this at some point if it is getting in the way of the therapy.

Some of the commonly used abbreviations are:

LOL	laugh out loud, or sharing the joke
BTW	by the way
IOW	in other words
BRB	be right back
AFAIK	as far as I know
EOM	end of message
HTH	hope this helps
IMS	I'm sorry
Thx	thanks
RU	for 'are you' e.g. in RUOK = are you OK
Pls	please
URW	you are welcome

Just be mindful of the fact that if you are working with a client whose first language is not English, an abbreviation may be used differently. For example, TOK would be 't'es OK?' and mrc would be 'merci' if used by, or to, a native French speaker.

The example given below demonstrates how a therapeutic conversation online might be conducted. It is shown in black type, more will be said later about the use of colour.

> Mona says:
> As I said last session, I am due to start a promotion within the company soon. It is the constant chain of events which follow me around that unsettle my mind, and I feel unable to cope.
> Anne says:
> Can you say a bit more about the chain of events?
> Mona says:
> I can't understand why this is happening. I now isolate myself almost completely and I spend most of my time alone.
> Mona says:
> I can't sleep and my appetite has been affected. I don't trust anyone.
> Mona says:
> It's a mess isn't it? LOL
> Anne says:
> So there's the concern over the promotion, what's happened in the past (that chain of events) . . .
> Anne says:
> Isolating yourself, the effect on your well-being, and that sense of not trusting anyone . . .
> Anne says:
> Have I got that right?
> Mona says:
> Absolutely – and when I see it laid out like that, I feel overwhelmed and don't know where to start to make a change in how things are. It just feels totally overwhelming.
> Anne says:
> Thinking about what you've said here . . .
> Anne says:
> If one thing could happen to make life seem less of a mess and less overwhelming at the moment, what would it be?

Mona says:

Gulp – I don't know. Let me think.

(Long pause without any sign of typing)

Mona says:

Sorry about the paws. I was thinking that maybe I need to try to see more of my friends. Then I would feel less isolated, and perhaps it would give me some head space when I wasn't dwelling on the promotion. Might sleep better if I do more in the evenings and week-ends too, but it feels daunting.

Anne says:

(I wasn't sure whether to check that you were OK, but didn't want to disturb your thinking.) How would it be . . .

Mona says:

Oh just thought when I read that, may be that's what's happening to my friends to – like they don't want to disturb me – they are not ringing me as much now – I think I've put them of – and yet I do want them to talk to me and show me they are still their.

Anne says:

So it would have been better if I had checked with you in the silence?

Mona says:

Yes! Oops that feels a bit rude!

Anne says:

LOL! feels fine at this end. I can't know if you don't tell me, and may be it's helped us to know what you might want to do, to help those feelings of being alone with it all.

This is purely a fictional exchange, but can be used to highlight some points about synchronous counselling. The client and the counsellor are shown here as using different font styles and sizes. This helps to differentiate who is speaking on the screen. It is often useful to use different colours as well. It makes therapeutic sense for the counsellor always to use one style, size and colour in all sessions with a particular client so that there is a sense of continuity for the client, and no 'out-of-awareness' wondering if something about the counsellor has changed. Changes in these things on the client's part may have some significance. For example, if they suddenly started using red when normally they use green, could it mean that anger is being surfaced? However, it is also important not to jump to conclusions as it may simply be that the client has been enjoying experimenting with the appearance of the text on the screen.

In this exchange, the counsellor does not use an emoticon until after Mona has done so, but does risk an abbreviation (LOL!) in response when Mona appears to be smiling about possibly sounding rude, as she had used 'oops', which sounds light-hearted.

The counsellor initially asked about the chain of events, but as Mona's response ignored that, a summary was used to try to find out what was the main issue of concern at present. Notice the use of 'Have I got that right?' This enables the client to correct the counsellor if necessary, and replaces the interrogatory tone of voice that might be used in f2f work, during the summary.

The sense of being overwhelmed is coming through strongly, so the counsellor decides to try to untangle some of this by asking what one thing would help. This resulted in a long silence in which it was obvious that Mona was not typing any response. This might create a number of reactions in the counsellor, from 'Oh help; was that the wrong intervention?' through a desire to rescue the client by breaking the silence, to panic that the client had simply gone away from the session.

In this case, because Mona has said that she needed to think, the counsellor decides just to stay with the silence and trust the process. It did result in Mona then being able to articulate something she felt would be useful, and the counsellor then in her response uses brackets to note her uncertainty about the silence. The use of brackets shows one form of using self-disclosure and/or immediacy in a manner that allows the client to ignore it if necessary.

In fact, this was what Mona responded to and the counsellor decided to stay with that and not complete the sentence that she had been formulating – or rather to delete it from the typing box and not press send. You may have noticed that the climate of the interaction seems to change at that point. Mona appears more engaged; there are more 'typos', which suggest she is trying to speak quickly and less formally. The first 'typo' occurred in the word 'paws' for 'pause'. That may have been simply a typing error, or there may have been something else going on. What does the word 'paws' mean to Mona? Does she have a pet that had come to join her at that moment? If the counsellor had followed this up at this stage, she would have been following her own agenda, rather than the client's. However, after the session or in supervision, she might chose to reflect on what it could have meant.

In some places, both client and counsellor have used a mechanism to speed up their words being read by the other. Instead of typing all they wished to say in one go, they typed part of their response and added a dotted line, pressed send so that those words were on the screen, and continued with the rest of what they wanted to say. If the client is not used to using online conversations, then before you begin working with them, you might consider giving them some 'tips' in a friendly sounding attachment which will help them to get through the learning stage of working this way.

For counsellors who use homework or tasks between f2f sessions, there would be an opportunity to do this with Mona. Mona could send an email to you setting out the chain of events that follow her around. You could ask her to look at the list of things that were overwhelming her and to prioritize them. If you use scaling in f2f work, Mona could be asked to keep a scaled diary of how overwhelmed she felt each day, and then in a future session you could look at what had made differences in the various points she had marked.

Depending on your counselling approach, you may want to evaluate the sessions as you go along. This could be as simple as reminding the client that the session is drawing to a close, and asking them what they have got out of today's work together, or what they found useful or unhelpful. You could adapt questions you use at the end of an f2f session to use online.

You might prefer to contract with the client that after each session you will send them an email asking for feedback. In this case, you might devise a simple form that asks perhaps three or four questions, for example as below.

Evaluation

- What did I (or we) do that helped today?
- Was there anything that was less helpful or unhelpful?
- Was there anything else you would have liked?
- Is there anything else you would like to say about our session?

Many counsellors will want to evaluate the work at the end of the contract. Again, this could be done synchronously as part of a final session or an email attachment could be sent to the client after the work has finished. Doing an evaluation as part of a live session allows it to be a two-way interactive process. However, it may mean that some clients stay with the positives and do not give you helpful developmental feedback. On the other hand, it does at least mean that there is some feedback. Clients do not always respond to an email after they have finished working with you. You may have to judge which method is more likely to be productive with a particular client.

In this chapter, the advantages and disadvantages of synchronous counselling have been considered, as well as some indications of how you might conduct a live session. Nothing prepares you as well as actually trying it out for yourself. The activities below are designed to help you do this.

Practice activities

1   If you are not used to using synchronous communication, download a free service such as Hotmail (www.hotmail.com) and sign up for a new email account. After you have done this, click on the MSN Messenger service. This will instruct you in how to set this up. Then practise talking online to friends who are already using this way of keeping in touch. (Ask a young person, as many of them do this all the time with their friends!)

2   If you already use live chat, or once you have completed activity 1, ask a counselling colleague to role-play an online client with you. At this point ask the colleague to keep the presenting issue fairly straightforward, as you are getting used to working online rather than wanting therapeutically deep issue. Ask for feedback from your colleague.

3   Either ask the same colleague if they would be prepared to reverse roles, so that you can experience what it is like to be an online client, or sign up for one or more sessions with an online counsellor who offers synchronous sessions. You can use the web search which you may have carried out after reading Chapter 3, or visit the ACTO website, http://www.acto-uk.org.

Chapter 6

Using Text to Explore Feelings

So far we have seen that online counselling occupies a niche where written words (text) distinguish it from other forms of counselling (e.g. f2f or telephone). This chapter shows how you can work with words therapeutically online. There is space here only for an overview and demonstration of how two of the many different writing tasks might be used. Books such as Adams (1990) or Progoff (1992) show many more. In this chapter we also demonstrate how a narrative approach can be used with online clients.

Before you introduce any writing task into the counselling work it is sensible to check that the client really wants to do one. They might decide that such a task puts them under even more pressure because it reminds them of school and failure. Such thoughts may make these tasks unnecessarily difficult, especially if they are working on them alone or as a homework task. Some clients prefer to do the therapeutic work when you are present in a live session, and it is possible to adapt the tasks described here so they can be completed either synchronously or asynchronously. Whichever way your client is working, it is sensible to suggest the task as a possibility rather than a necessary part of the work, and they may or may not choose to do it. A preliminary email might say:

Now that you have described what you would like to look at in counselling, one way of approaching the work might be through some therapeutic writing. I notice that you write fluently and have different ways of describing yourself and the situation you find yourself in now. Therapeutic writing can be a powerful and effective tool which gets in touch with hidden feelings and brings them into conscious awareness where they can be examined. However, you will need to feel supported both in your everyday life and by our relationship to make the most of such tasks because the work can be painful but the reward is usually peace of mind and a greater resourcefulness for dealing with future problems. If, having read this, you have strong feelings against doing such tasks, I will respect your choice and we can, of course, continue as we are.

THERAPEUTIC WRITING TASKS

One important aspect of any writing task is to share the writing with someone who will not judge its quality but who will act as a witness and validate the writer's experience. If you are working synchronously in live sessions, the writing can be done either during the session or sent as an email before the session (if it was set as a homework task). Working asynchronously on a writing task (through email or message board), you can ask clients to send you the writing by email instead of reading it out loud and you can witness and validate their writing in your email reply, telling them how it moved you as the reader. Another feature of working online asynchronously is that you can encourage the client to notice and discuss their feelings on doing the task, and to include this in their email response (you may also want to do this in a live session). The therapeutic email for the client then falls into two parts. In one part they present their therapeutic writing and in the second part they stand back from it and give you an objective view of its usefulness, together with a description of any 'here and now' feelings they experienced when doing the task. This two-part approach (the task and the accompanying feelings) encourages both client and counsellor to notice and explore therapeutically the feelings evoked by the writing.

When a client agrees to do a writing task, it is good practice to send them not only the proposed task, which can be adapted and tailored specifically to the issue, but also some more general instructions for completing it. These instructions must be clear and take the writer from the very beginning to the very end of the task. The task will be done in an isolated situation and good instructions can help the client to prepare for, and manage, the strong feelings that might be stirred. Some clients become caught up in their feelings and will complete the task in one burst of energy, then send it immediately, without re-reading or editing; others will write in smaller chunks over a longer period. The action of writing itself becomes part of a cathartic experience as they describe issues that concern them.

Here is an example of some instructions for completing a writing task:

Completing a therapeutic writing task

Allow 30–40 uninterrupted minutes.
- Sit at your computer and think for a minute or two about what the task is
- Open a blank page on your computer
- Put the heading '...'
- Type all thoughts/ideas/words as they come into your head
- Carry on until you have finished
- Send to me without editing or re-writing (unless you wish to do this)
- Give yourself a 'reward' (bath, walk, glass of wine, turn on music/TV, read a book)

If you can't get started after about 10 minutes,
- Save the Word document somewhere private (removable disk? pass-worded file?)
- Give yourself a reward as above – for making a start

If you have started but left it unfinished,
- Read it through another time and decide if you want to add more
- When it is completed click Send
- Give yourself a reward as above

Some writing tasks lend themselves readily to emails. They range from descriptive/reflective tasks such as memories (of childhood, a loved one, a time in their lives), dreams or significant moments in the past. Other types of therapeutic writing become the email itself. Two of these are described below.

UNSENT LETTERS

When a client appears to have strong feelings about an issue which they want to explore but can't quite put their feelings into words, an 'unsent letter' may be a good way to access such feelings and explore their meaning. For example, a client may be feeling very sad and hopeless about the death of someone close to them or they may have a powerful feeling of rage towards someone or something. One way of working with this would be to suggest that they try a piece of therapeutic writing to explore their feelings about the issue further. You invite them to write an unsent letter (UL) to the person or thing that is causing the feeling, saying all the unsayable, unspeakable thoughts and words that come into their head. (Our clients have written in this way to Chemotherapy, Painful Back, Body, Money, Alcohol, Little Me, etc.) Whether the UL is directed to a person or a body part, they begin by writing 'Dear ....' as if they are writing to a person. They don't edit their writing but send it just as it comes out (ULs have ranged from a list of words or phrases to pages of unparagraphed writing which may or may not be divided into sentences). The more fractured and disjointed the typing and the language become, the closer they are to getting into touch with their inner feelings about the email's recipient. When the UL is finished, they send it as an email to you, their counsellor. Sometimes a single UL will be enough to enable the client to express what they have not been able to express in words. Your task will be to validate the feelings and help the client to explore any new thoughts they have discovered since writing.

Other clients may find it useful to send and respond to a UL in a series of emails using the structure below.

Three Unsent Letter Emails

1   The client writes a UL to whatever is concerning them. They send their UL as a file attachment and in the covering email tell the counsellor how they felt as they began the task and how they are feeling now they have got the words out of their head and down in writing (some counsellors like to use scales for measuring clients' feelings). The counsellor may choose to act briefly as a witness to the UL, validating their experience and telling the client of any relevant thoughts or emotions it evoked in them, or they may prefer to stand to one side and continue with the task, reserving their comments for when it is completed.

2   The counsellor copies and pastes the client's UL into the body of the email and invites them to imagine they have just received the UL below, suggesting they write a response to the sender and send it back as before. When the letter is moved into an email, the text looks different to the client because line endings and any formatting they may have used will have changed and the client is more likely to read it all through once again before replying.

3   The client writes back as the original UL recipient, attaching their UL to the email and telling the counsellor how they are feeling now.

4   The counsellor copies their second UL back into their reply and asks the client to write a reply as themselves.

This email dialogue can go on as long as it seems useful, but three emails are often sufficient for the client to have gained some insight that helps them view their situation in a new light. At the end of this series of UL emails, the counsellor validates what the client has experienced in completing the task and facilitates them to explore and notice any changes that have happened as a result.

In this way, ULs become sent and the writer has a chance to receive and read what they have written in a setting that is both safe and realistic for the task. They also know that their writing has been shared and their experience validated and witnessed by someone else.

WORKING WITH DIALOGUE

Another type of therapeutic writing which can be used with clients both asynchronously and synchronously is to dialogue (Adams, 1990; Progoff, 1992) with an aspect of themselves or their current lives that is causing them a problem. Most dialogues we have worked on with clients have been written between an aspect of the client's personality which is hidden or oppressed and a more public aspect such as 'Confident Me' and 'Unconfident Me' or 'Wise Me' and 'Foolish Me'. However, dialogues can be written between the client and an 'Inner Child', 'Inner Wisdom' (often externalized as a 'Wise Person'), 'Parent' ('Critical' or 'Nurturing'), 'Boss', or an important aspect of their lives such as 'Work' or 'Money'.

USING DIALOGUE ASYNCHRONOUSLY

Before beginning to write a dialogue we suggest that our online clients read a Dialogue Meditation (Adams, 1990) such as the example below. This frees the conscious mind and makes it more receptive to the words and thoughts from both parties in the dialogue.

Dialogue meditation (*please read through before beginning your dialogue*)

Sit back in your chair
Take your hands away from the keyboard
Relax and take three slow breaths
Imagine it is a warm sunny day and you are walking to meet . . . (*your dialogue partner*)
Notice the sounds you can hear around you,
The feel of the warm sunshine
You can see . . . in the distance
They are too far away to see clearly but they are walking towards you
You walk towards each other
You can see . . . clearly now
You are close enough to talk
You stop and look at each other
You know that you can ask any question and you will be answered
You can make any statement and you will be heard

Dialogues are written as conversations, with each new voice on a new line (see below). Clients are invited to write the dialogue as a Word document attached to an email. In the email they describe anything they noticed about themselves while completing the task. These 'here and now' descriptions help online counsellors to understand how the client is responding to the task, particularly if strong feelings are evoked. It is suggested that they can continue the dialogue for as long as seems useful, or they might prefer to set an alarm to go off after 30 minutes so that they can assess whether to take a break or continue for a bit longer.

Here is part of a fictitious dialogue in which 'Inner Me' (IM) is discussing an issue with 'Outer Me' (OM).

IM: I get paralysed by you. I can't say what I want to say, you don't listen. I can't think about things I want to think about because you're always planning the future and solving day-to-day problems.

OM: Look, I know you're there all the time but you never have anything useful to say. You're such a dreamer, you never have any plans for our future or any practical solutions to problems. I do all that.

IM: How will you ever know if I've got plans if you never let me speak?

OM: Well, OK, I'm letting you speak now and I'm listening.

IM: It's really hard to put things into words just like that. Sometimes I feel so scared of everything I want to curl up and hide.

OM: I do know when you're scared – it scares me, too. I feel I have to be the strong one and protect us from danger and that's hard to do.

IM: We're both scared sometimes.

OM: Guess we are.

IM: I didn't realize that. I thought you found it easy to be the strong one – fighting for us, arguing with people, always getting your own way.

OM: Sometimes I wanted someone to take care of me and not allow me to get away with things.

IM: That's how I feel most of the time and a lot of the time you do that, you do take care of me and not allow me to get away with things. I didn't realize it wasn't what you wanted.

OM: I can be scared too, you know. Funny, we're both talking about being scared but it doesn't feel a scary thing to do, at least it doesn't to me.

IM: I agree, I would have thought if we were both scared it would be even scarier but it isn't. I feel a lot closer to you now we've started talking like this.

OM: I feel I know you better, too. Perhaps that's why it doesn't seem so scary. Perhaps we're feeling stronger because we are on the same wavelength, thinking the same things and feeling the same way. We should talk like this again.

IM: Yes, it's been very helpful. We will do it again and again. When we're thinking together, it feels as if we don't need to be afraid of anything out there.

USING DIALOGUE IN A SYNCHRONOUS SESSION

Dialogues can also be used in a live session where the counsellor addresses an aspect of the client if both of them agree that it would be appropriate. Such a task forms only a part of the session; the counsellor needs to be aware of the time and not introduce the idea of a dialogue too late in the session as there has to be sufficient time both for the dialogue and for discussing it and debriefing afterwards. If there is an opening for a dialogue late in a session it could become a homework task using the instructions above. Dialogues and post-dialogue discussions generally take at least 30 minutes.

Before the dialogue can begin, the counsellor and client clarify who the dialogue is with, the issue to be explored and what part the counsellor will play in it. The counsellor will usually talk directly to the 'person' or 'strong feeling' the client wants to explore, asking them about their part in the client's life. The extract below is a fictitious synchronous session with a client. Here, both client and counsellor have already agreed that the counsellor will address the client's child (Little C) and the counsellor has just asked what Little C would like to talk about. The counsellor simplifies her language and repeats back the words and phrases the client uses in order to facilitate talking to Little C, addressing her directly. The counsellor also uses the present tense even when the client uses the past tense to assist the client to experience being Little C again.

> Client: Little C is wondering about her judgement of other people and her instinct, and whether these have been flawed all her life or whether her confidence just allowed her to slip a little. Other people didn't like me and I didn't know what I was doing wrong.
> **Counsellor: Little C, can you tell me a bit more about this?**
> Client: I can't trust my instincts at all. I mistrust everybody until they prove themselves to me. It's the only way I am safe. I think I am making it hard for people to like me.
> **Counsellor: How are you making it hard for people to like you?**
> Client: I don't give anything of myself away. At first, I'm quite cold and distant until I feel safe enough. I don't have many friends. But a few people stayed with me long enough for me to relax and show my real self.
> **Counsellor: Little C, why do you think some people stay long enough for you to show your real self?**
> Client: Most didn't. Don't know why they stayed perhaps they were concerned for me.
> **Counsellor: You don't sound very sure about that.**

Client: I don't think they were and I also remember many people didn't like Little C and said so.

Counsellor: How does Little C feel about that?

Client: She is very unhappy. She's lonely and only has a few friends.

Counsellor: What does Little C want to happen?

Client: I want some more friends too many people hate me it's not fair!

Counsellor: Is Little C feeling lonely?

Client: Yes, but I'm not going to let people see how lonely I am.

Counsellor: Little C is hiding her feelings. She doesn't show what she is really feeling.

Client: Yes, I became very clever at hiding how I really felt.

Counsellor: And is Little C still hiding her feelings away from other people?

Client: Yes, it's the only safe thing to do.

Counsellor: Does Little C want to say some more about hiding her feelings?

Client: Perhaps, but not right now. I feel very tired suddenly.

Counsellor: And I'm aware that our time is drawing to a close – it seems important for us to discuss how you are feeling as C before we leave this session.

Client: I feel quite drained and exhausted, I hadn't realized how I hid things away even when I was young. I need time to think about this and to re-read what I said – the words just seemed to come out by themselves, I didn't feel in charge of my fingers or my brain.

Counsellor: It can be a very powerful exercise. Do you think it was useful?

Client: Yes, in spite of feeling tired I feel lighter somehow, as though a weight has been lifted. Maybe this is an important discovery I've just made – not sure if it is, or how it will be useful yet.

Counsellor: It did seem as though you were saying something very important. I was feeling more alert than usual when you were writing as Little C – I found myself staring at the screen, unable to look away in case I missed something. As I say, it's a very powerful exercise. Is there anything else you would like to say here?

Client: Not really, I'm yawning away and it's only 8 pm! I think I'll go and get a glass of wine and have some quiet time to myself now. See you next week as usual and thanks for this week.

Counsellor: That glass of wine sounds like a good idea. See you next week. Bye and take care.

Client: I will. Bye.

You can see from this example that the client moves quite suddenly out of speaking as Little C. The counsellor realizes this and moves into discussion of the dialogue rather than continuing to address Little C. During the discussion the counsellor acts as a witness, validating the client's experience and disclosing any relevant feelings of their own. Dialogues like these can be brief segments of a synchronous session or can take up the majority of a session. The intensity of the feelings and the sense of having a third 'person' in the session is very strong and there is a need to acknowledge that shared experience. Just as with the email therapeutic writing tasks, counsellors may suggest that clients give themselves a treat following an online session. It is good practice to do this because there is no break for the client from being in a counselling session to being in their daily life. There is no journey from the counsellor's office to home and no time to reflect on the session before their daily world resumes.

As with all online counselling, the counsellor needs to be constantly aware of the environment in which the counselling is taking place. They should introduce exercises such as the ones here with care and with awareness of how the client might be feeling both as a result of doing the exercise and how it may affect them immediately afterwards, when they resume their daily life.

Practice activity

Creative Writing

If you haven't done so already, set up a new email address with Hotmail or Yahoo for yourself as an online counsellor.

- Imagine your online counsellor has suggested you write an 'unsent letter' to someone who is significant in your life.
- Using the instructions in this chapter, write the unsent letter and email it to 'your' online counsellor.
- In the covering email describe how you felt both as you wrote the unsent letter and after you clicked the Send icon.
- Collect the unsent letter from your counsellor email address.
- Write a response as the counsellor encouraging the client to continue with a further letter, if appropriate.

USING A NARRATIVE APPROACH IN THERAPY

Another form of writing that lends itself to online counselling is narrative, in which the exchanges (whether synchronous or asynchronous) are treated as a continuing and developing narrative between counsellor and client (McLeod, 1997; Payne, 2000). White and Epston's (1990) work in Australia translates well into online therapy; indeed, these authors are applying their techniques online now. Their model consists of four stages. Initially the counsellor helps the client to identify and externalize the client's problem (separates the problem from the person) then helps them to discover the parts of their story that have 'unique outcomes' (client behaviours that had unexpectedly successful results). The counsellor then helps the client to re-author and 'proclaim' (tell others) their story. The counsellor witnesses the client's movement from a problem-dominated to a problem-managed narrative. This model works well online since the counselling is permanently recorded in text. Online counsellors can help the client to externalize the problem (perhaps suggesting they give their problem a name, putting it for example as the subject line of emails). Online counsellors can draw attention to unique outcomes and encourage the client to re-author their story and proclaim it. For example a counsellor might write:

> I'm sitting here with a smile on my face. I see from your last email how differently you are thinking about your father now. In your early emails you called him Bully (your email No. 2 was headed 'Bully Gets His Way') and in it you gave a painful account of how he 'dominated you by shouting and lashing out with his fists'. Then you described in email No. 4 how he unexpectedly agreed with you one time because you shouted back at him but you were disappointed that this didn't last long. But in this email (No. 8) you say he was 'someone who had to shout to get his own way because it was the only way he could feel important'. Sounds like your view of him has changed. Have I got that right? As well as being pleased for your new understanding I'm puzzling over what made the difference – was it writing those unsent letters to him or was it our emails about you? Can you help me understand what made the difference? We began our emails with a problem which doesn't seem to be a problem any more!

As narrative theory recommends, externalizing the problem is a good way to begin to deconstruct the client's 'problem-dominated' story. Any work with the client on giving the problem a name, using the name of the problem as a title for emails or an unsent letter (as described earlier in this chapter) helps the client to begin this externalization process. For some clients, treating their emails as chapters in a book with the chapter title in the subject line of the email is also effective here. In synchronous work externalization can be achieved by giving a name or a title to each session, either at the beginning or at the end, whichever is more appropriate.

Using the therapeutic email exchanges as chapter titles in a book helps clients by breaking down their experience into more manageable segments. They can free their minds of the jumble of information they've been trying to hold on to and reconstruct it in an order that is meaningful to them. For example:

Chapter 1	My earliest memories
Chapter 2	Friends and relatives
Chapter 3	Challenges I have faced
Chapter 4	Mistakes I've made
Chapter 5	Things I regret
Chapter 6	Learning about myself
Chapter 7	New things I want to try

As the client writes each chapter, they describe whatever is evoked by the chapter title. In response, the counsellor acts as a witness to the writing and validates what the client has described. Counsellors may also work therapeutically with the text, using a mix of questioning, challenge and therapeutic writing tasks to encourage the client to explore the wider aspects of their experience. They help them to discover unique outcomes (times when they didn't respond to an experience in the way they thought they would) and finally helping them to reconstruct and proclaim their story (by sending it to you, and you encouraging them to tell someone close to them when they are ready).

Another way a counsellor can help the client to reconstruct their story is to encourage them to tell their story from a different point of view:

> This has been a very powerful experience for you and it seems still to be powerful. Sometimes it helps people who are stuck with strong feelings about an experience to describe the event again but from the point of view of the other person who was there at the time. Perhaps it would help you if you wrote to me about what happened but from the point of

view of the friend who was with you. Let him describe it all to me. What would he have noticed? How would he describe the experience that has caused you such pain ever since? Perhaps your next therapeutic email could be from him.

Online narrative therapy can help a client face issues that they may have avoided facing in real life. Their avoidance might be due to shame, fear, guilt or some other negative view that they hold about themselves and/or the issue. By using the supportive relationship and relative anonymity offered by online counselling, they can separate themselves from the issue, then explore, examine and reconstruct it or put it in a new context.

Practice activity

Narrative Therapy

Describe your life as a series of chapters in a book – give each chapter a heading. Write about one of the chapters and email it to your online counsellor putting the title of the chapter as the subject line.

Notice how this feels.
• Visit your online counselling address and open the email.
• Write a reply to it in the role of witness, validating what has been written and encouraging the writer to continue with another chapter.

SUMMARY

Online counselling has a special relationship with text, and written words form a unique channel through which it is conducted. The physical action of typing the words together with re-reading and seeing their permanence on the screen all help the client by adding strength and force to what they say. Writing tasks help the client to identify and clarify their story and feelings, and to explore, confront, evaluate and challenge previously held views. In doing this, they can say the unsayable, release previously hidden feelings and share their deepest concerns about an issue that is troubling them. The online counselling relationship supports them while they are doing the work. Research has shown that the client may construct an 'idealized' therapist in their own mind (Goss and Anthony, 2003) and the relationship they experience with this ideal therapist helps to support them as they work on their own at their own computer.

Practice activity

Practice Ideas when using Therapeutic Writing tasks

- Assess the client's willingness to participate with some therapeutic writing before suggesting any tasks.
- Provide adequate written instructions that are clear and simple to follow.
- Use formatting (e.g. bulleted lists) for different stages of the task.
- Make suggestions for self-soothing after the therapeutic writing has ended.

Chapter 7

Working Therapeutically Online with Image and Sound

One of the features of computers and the internet is the ease with which image and sound files can be created, stored and sent to other computers. In the first part of this chapter we discuss some of the ways in which image and sound can be used in online counselling and in the second part we give some practical information about how image and sound can be created, saved, stored and sent from one computer to another.

The rationale for using image or sound in online work may be a combination of counsellor training and their client's preferences. If a client describes themselves in a very visual way or sends pictures or links to songs or asks for audio or audiovisual sessions, they may like to work this way. Some online counsellors use image or sound as additional therapeutic tools only with clients who show they are receptive to this way of working, others include image and sound as part of their normal therapeutic practice.

USING CREATIVE ARTS THERAPY ONLINE

When both audio and video contact are available, online counselling can take on a new dimension as both client and therapist see and hear each other. Creative Arts Therapy (CAT) involves all the performing arts (music, dance, drama, art, poetry, etc.) and can take full advantage of the possibilities of computer-mediated image and sound. Alex Chew (a colleague at Counselling Online Ltd) has used this approach in his work with online clients for a number of years. His clients' technology skills and confidence may vary and initially Alex assesses and explores the client's computer knowledge and confidence as well as their suitability for this type of therapeutic work. He can adapt his work to fit the client's level of computer competence. If the client has no broadband connection, for example, the work can be done asynchronously using email, or live sessions could be held using VoIP (Skype) or an instant messenger whiteboard. Those with confidence and broadband can work with him in a website area which Alex can prepare beforehand and tailor to the client's needs. In CAT the whiteboard (a blank screen with drawing tools – see Glossary) becomes a shared space between therapist and client where both can work together. One CAT whiteboard might show three boxes, one of which is empty and the therapist invites the client to fill it. Another might have a series of cartoon pictures with empty speech bubbles and the client is invited to add the words and complete the story. Whiteboard images can be saved and stored on the participants' computers for further work or review at a later time. A picture of a whiteboard is shown later in this chapter.

When therapists are using a CAT approach they use relaxation and visualization exercises at the start of a session to free the client's unconscious brain. Online, a synchronous relaxation and visualization exercise requires a mixture of audio and visual connection through a webcam (a computer camera) because the therapist needs to see the client and observe their breathing in order to assess when the the client is relaxed and ready to undertake a therapeutic task. One such task might be, for example, to draw what they see using their non-dominant hand to connect with their childhood feelings. Online, the therapist invites the client to draw on a piece of paper at the side of their computer and hold the picture up to their webcam for the therapist to see. The therapist encourages the client to connect with their inner child, inviting them to talk about the feelings the picture evokes and create a nurturing or re-parenting experience. The example below shows a non-dominant-hand drawing called 'when I was happy'. The client added that as a child her only happy memories were of walking her dog and getting away from her home where she was bullied and bossed around by older siblings.

Another use of the whiteboard might be to create a story using randomly selected pictures (available on the British Dramatherapy website www.badth.org.uk). The client chooses six cards which are used one at a time in the session to build a six-part monomyth (Joseph Campbell's description of the basic heroic story found in many narratives from around the world, e.g. the stories of Buddah, Moses and Christ). Depending on how the client develops the story and what self-destructive themes are included, the therapist introduces reparative experiences through mutual story-telling which can be spoken if the client has a microphone or otherwise typed on the whiteboard chatscreen. Another option is for both therapist and client to construct a story (either typed or using audio) with the therapist generating options when the client takes the story to a single outcome that seems to have no way forward.

WORKING WITH IMAGE ONLINE

Some clients both think and express themselves more easily in image than in words, and if the online counsellor senses this is the case they may choose to use image in the work both to provide an eloquent substitution for the words and to enhance them. Images such as photographs evoke memories and access feelings that may have been suppressed since the time the photograph was taken. Watching a repeat of a favourite film on DVD or TV can remind the viewer of previous times when they viewed it as well as the feelings that the film evokes now. Drawing symbolic representations of family members on a whiteboard (see example later in this chapter) can reveal aspects of these relationships that might not otherwise be part of the therapy.

Images can be created using paints, crayons, objects suitable for collage or other art materials. The experience of using these simple materials reminds clients of their childhood, and this releases creativity which might have been lost when growing up. An image can by-pass conscious feelings and defence mechanisms to work on unconscious experiences and memories through the feelings it evokes. An image can bring out what was forgotten or unsayable at the time, adding depth and bringing a wider perspective to an issue, perhaps a memory of a disturbing event or experience from the past or a disturbing pattern of response in the present. Therapists who work with image might encourage their clients to send images that are relevant to the work they are doing by email as a file attachment which can be discussed with them in a live session when they are both viewing the image on their respective computer screens.

Photographs (particularly those taken in childhood) are useful in therapy and can be shared over the internet by scanning the actual photograph and turning it into a digital file. The digital file can then be opened, stored and sent from one computer to another. Digital photography also makes sharing photographs very easy after they are scaled down to a suitable size (see file re-sizing). Photographs can be used in a variety of ways and Judy Weiser's book (Weiser, 1999) is full of suggestions that could be used online as well as in the f2f setting. In her therapeutic practice, photographs are used to assist clients to access unconscious feelings that may have been repressed. By bringing them into the conscious therapeutic space they may be explored, understood differently (with the perspective of time) and changed so that they no longer create emotional 'no go' areas. When working in this way as a therapist, Weiser suggests that her input is restricted to a natural curiosity, coupled with a lack of assumptions or leading questions. This can encourage the client to explore the reasons behind their choice of image and discover their own meanings and viewpoints. Any links the therapist notices can be brought into later discussions once the client has discovered new meanings.

During a pilot for an online course on Working with Image, the course tutor invited course members to send images that represented 'a quality I have inherited or a quality I would dislike my children to inherit' or an image which they associated with 'sadness, joy, calm or anger'. Here is one of them.

The group member who sent in the image said in discussion:

> I hope my children will be like this tree and not be afraid to stand out from the crowd and stick to what they believe is important. I was more like the other trees in this picture when I was younger, happier blending into the landscape. I used to ignore my ideas and go along with the ideas of more persuasive friends so I didn't stick out. I even used to tell myself that I was the one the one who'd got it wrong. I know now that sometimes I'd got it right!

Practice activity

Find a picture or photograph that represents 'a quality I have inherited or one that I would not want my children to inherit from me' and send it as an email to your 'Counsellor' email address, with a few words about how it is significant.

In individual therapy, images are shared with the counsellor and the emotional decisions and background issues that went into their choice can become the focus for a therapeutic discussion. Counsellors may want to have a selection of useful images available on their website for clients to choose from (a collection that could be tailored to the purposes of therapy) or they may suggest that clients search the internet to find images for themselves if they do not wish to restrict client choice.

SECOND LIFE AND OTHER VIRTUAL REALITY COMMUNITIES

Another internet platform using image and sound, with therapeutic uses, is the virtual reality community, the most popular of which is Second Life. Other virtual reality communities are found in online games, particularly those that involve roleplay. Virtual reality has been in use for some time as an educational tool. In the medical and aviation industries surgeons and pilots have used virtual reality simulators to rehearse complicated operations or to learn how to use new tools. This technology was later developed for leisure use by the games industry.

The development of sophisticated virtual reality communities which are accessible online, of which the most active is probably Second Life (http://www.secondlife.com), has provided new possible sources of clients for online counsellors, some of whom have opened virtual offices in Second Life. In order to enter the virtual community of Second Life, visitors download the free program and select an avatar (see Glossary) which will represent them. The avatar's movements and gestures are controlled through the keyboard and they are free move around a computer screen world of Second Life residents, interacting by chatscreen or voice as they choose. Second Life is not an online game (although at first sight it may look like one to a visitor) the following quotation taken from *Second Life for Dummies* (Robbins and Bell, 2008, p. 11) describes its purpose as follows: 'So exactly what do you do in Second Life? Well, you live a *second* life. Anything you can do in real life (from washing dishes and buying a house to getting a job and getting married) you can do in SL.' The picture below shows two avatars in a virtual world (in fact it is the setting where one of the avatars conducts counselling sessions).

Clients can use this virtual community to rehearse and practise new behaviours. Cognitive behavioural therapists have found that Second Life is very useful for clients who are ready to confront phobias or anxieties (e.g. social anxiety), either doing this as a homework task and reporting back to their therapist or confronting their phobias in a live session with their therapist in the therapist's Second Life office. Other counsellors who are working therapeutically with clients using Second Life are finding that the work is not restricted to this approach, and work with their clients in ways that are similar to those used in real-world settings. It is believed that online disinhibition, anonymity and control of all aspects of their avatar, from the way it looks to where it goes, free clients to reveal aspects of themselves that might be inaccessible in the real world.

Therapists who are Second Life residents might use their office to create a fantasy world with obstacles (such as a creative arts therapist might use for a therapeutic journey with their client) or fill an empty chair with a third avatar (who is significant in the client's life) who can be 'present' in the session, or accompany their client while they confront their worst fears. In any event, the counsellor can tailor each setting specifically to the client.

In addition to the therapeutic ways in which a virtual community such as Second Life can be used, virtual reality communities can also provide empowering experiences for some people who feel disadvantaged in real life (e.g. through physical disability, communication problems, etc.). An avatar which they have chosen themselves and whose characteristics are entirely under their control can help them tolerate their real-life disability (physical or emotional, visible or invisible) in a more resourceful way. Online counsellors who work therapeutically with Second Life residents will need to be comfortable with the possibility that they may not only help these clients to confront and challenge areas of themselves that were previously hidden in the real world, but also that the significance of Second Life and real life might in fact be reversed. The focus of the therapy may not be to help clients re-integrate new understanding and insight back into real life (though that may also happen but not be discussed) so much as to help them deal with issues that only seem relevant to their Second Life avatar.

CREATING AND SHARING IMAGE AND SOUND FILES

On a practical level, working with image and sound needs a high level of computer confidence if it is to be useful. Where clients are less confident about using technology, counsellors may need to be technology educators as well. Images and sounds are created and stored as files on the computer and these files can be shared with other computers either synchronously (using a whiteboard, webcam, VoIP connection with audio headset) or asynchronously (by sending an image or sound file as an email attachment or sending a URL link in an email to a website where the sound or image can be played).

SIZING, SENDING AND RECEIVING IMAGE FILES

In order to work with image online it is important to understand how to re-size image files so that they can be sent over the internet (the larger the file, the longer it will take to arrive and the more chance there is that some parts of the file will be lost en route). Images can be sent during a synchronous session on Instant Messenger using the file-sharing facility of the Messenger program (which can sometimes be very slow) or via email as a file attachment (faster, but you need to have your email program open as well). Image files have various suffixes to show they are image files (.jpg, .tiff, .gif etc.), which denote how the data are sent. Jpg files, sometimes known as jpeg files, are a compressed format and offer the lowest file sizes.

Many image files are too large to send easily over the internet (it can take several minutes to download 1 Mb on a dialup internet connection) and the instructions below apply to all large image files. Most files need to be below 1 Mb if you want to send them by email and don't want them to tie up too much of your recipient's time downloading to their computer. To reduce an image file size, first open the image in a picture program such as Photoshop or Paint. Then choose Save As from the file menu and save the image as a jpg file (we recommend saving the image to your desktop so you can easily locate it again). When the file begins to save, you will be offered a choice of resolution (file size). Choose the

> **Tip**
>
> **Re-sizing image files**
>
> Open the image in a picture program (Photoshop, Paint, etc.)
>
> Choose File > Save As
>
> Name picture and select where to save it (e.g. desktop)
>
> Choose JPEG or .jpg from file menu
>
> Click OK
>
> Select smallest file size/lowest resolution
>
> Click OK

lowest if the picture is to be viewed on a computer screen, as this is quite adequate.

Images that can be sent online range from the emoticons found in most Instant Messenger chat programs (see Chapter 3) through hand-drawn or painted images to a photograph. A photographic image can be a digital photograph from your own camera or a printed photograph that has been scanned into a computer, or an image copied from a website. Theoretically anything on a website can be copied and saved to your computer (see instructions below). Ask permission of the website owner before you copy an image in case it is copyrighted. In practice this is seldom done, especially if the image is for personal use only. Some people use photographic and other images which they have found on image websites such as Google Image. These are freely available for anyone to use and are generally small files that will not need to be re-saved. (*To check a file size, right click on it and choose 'Properties' from the menu (Windows) or Cntrl+click and 'Get Info' (Mac).*)

> **Tip**
>
> **Saving an image from a website**
>
> 1 Right click on the image.
> 2 Choose 'Save Image as . . .' from the menu.
> 3 Name your image and choose where to save it (e.g. desktop).

WORKING WITH A SCANNER AND DIGITAL CAMERA

An image can also be obtained by scanning. These images could be printed photographs, hand-drawn or painted images on a piece of paper, or objects placed directly on to the glass of a scanner. (The scanning process turns the image into a file on your computer.) Most scanners have their own program for operating their scanning function and usually the most important decision you have to make is to tell the scanner where to save it on your computer. If you choose your computer's desktop you will be able to find the image file easily and from there you can open it in a picture program, re-size it as necessary and save it as described above.

In the same way, digital cameras are a useful source of images. Once you have saved them on your computer, the only adjustments to make before sharing them with someone else over the internet is to make sure the image file is of a suitable size.

WORKING WITH A WHITEBOARD

Whiteboards are a feature of many Instant Messenger programs (along with audio and webcam). While sitting at their individual computer screens, every participant in a Messenger conversation can access the whiteboard and use the tools to create a drawing or text. The tools allow any of the whiteboard participants to draw objects (such as a filled circle or square), use different colours for lines or shapes, hand-write or draw (with mouse) or type text. Some whiteboards also allow participants to copy and paste a small image onto them. Objects on the whiteboard can be moved around and re-sized as the participants choose, and text can be added. The example below shows a whiteboard session with a fictitious client where the client has drawn a family group with each member represented as a filled circle which is then named. The whiteboard tools used (filled circle and text) are shown along the top. In order to draw a filled circle, for example, the client selects the fill colour (black in this case) by clicking their mouse on the relevant colour (small blocks along the top); then clicks the filled circle to 'choose' it. To use the filled circle tool, they move the mouse to the whiteboard and click again (to activate the tool) then drag the mouse across the whiteboard until they have a circle of the size they want. To add the text, they select the text tool and the size of text from the drop-down menu. They click the whiteboard where they want the text to appear, and then type. Here is a screenshot of the whiteboard described above:

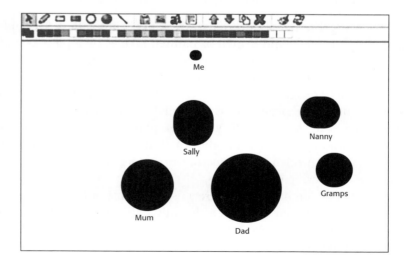

The counsellor and the client were meeting on Instant Messenger and communicating using the Messenger chatscreen. Here is an extract of what they discussed.

> Client: I think I've made myself very small... Sally got more attention than me . . .
> Client: she was sick a lot as a child so Nanny and Gramps would come and look after her if Dad was away and Mum was working . . .
> Client: Everyone was so busy.
>
> (*Long pause*)
> **Counsellor: Everyone was so busy. I notice you've put yourself at the edge of the picture.**
> Client: Yes . . . I felt on the edge . . . on the edge of the family that's a good way of putting it . . .
> Client: No one left me out deliberately but everyone fussed around Sally or Dad if he was coming home and I just felt left out of everything.

Practice activity

Imagine you are the counsellor in the above exchange. What homework task might you set the client at the end of the session?

WORKING WITH A WEBCAM AND VIDEO

Webcams (computer cameras) are also useful in therapy, not only to see each other, but to hold up images for the other person to see. This instant form of sharing can be useful during a synchronous session where a client may have prepared an image for homework or may be drawing the image by hand during the session (see earlier in this chapter). Live sessions on webcam are possible providing both counsellor and client accept the limitations of the video medium and are prepared for either image or sound or both, to fragment or disappear completely from time to time during a session. Some clients may make videos of themselves which they want to send to you or they may ask you to view other videos that have special meaning for them. These might need to be uploaded to a web-server that handles large files (see later in this chapter) or may be uploaded to a public website full of videos such as YouTube. In this way, the internet becomes a resource that can show you more aspects of the client than you might see in f2f counselling sessions.

SENDING AND RECEIVING SOUND FILES

Sound files can be sent and received in a similar way to image files. Sound can be shared live using an audio headset or by email using file attachments or URL links. One word of warning, people with dial-up internet connections may find live audio sessions can be beset with intrusive sounds and delays which can impair the quality of the session. If you have broadband yourself, you may want to check with your client to ensure that their connection speed is adequate if they want to have a live audio session with you.

Most computer systems will have a sound card installed, which means you can listen to sound but not necessarily record a sound file. You may need to explore what your computer has in the way of recording software if you want to do this. Sound files sent as an email file attachment must be small: the most commonly used file format for sharing such files is the compressed (mp3) format. Free programs can be downloaded from the internet to convert files from uncompressed sound formats (wav, .aiff or .au) into compressed ones such as .mp3 and search engines such as Google can locate these for you. Like image files, sound files can be very large unless they are in a suitably compressed format. Some clients may like to send actual recordings of themselves or a favourite song which has special meaning for them. Alternatively they may send the name of the song and perhaps a website link (URL) where it is performed so you can visit the website and listen to it yourself.

A live audio therapy session on Skype can be recorded using free software (downloaded from the Skype menu) and the recorded session can be converted into an .mp3 file and sent to the client as a reminder of what was said. However, if your recording is a long one (e.g. takes more than 10 minutes to play) it may not compress into a small enough file to send by email. Some ISPs have restrictions on the size of file they will accept. In such cases, you can upload your file to web servers which specialize in accepting large files (e.g. http://www.Pando.com or http://www.sendthis-file.com). After downloading their free software you can send (upload) your file to the web server, and give them the email address of the recipient. The bulk file web server sends an email to the recipient telling them there is a file waiting for them to collect and instructions for how to do this. Clearly there are issues about confidentiality if you send a therapy session in this way (it will be held on a web server awaiting collection and could be intercepted) and you may prefer to use an encryption web server such as Hushmail (see Chapter 4), which offers encrypted facilities for files of up to 15 Mb. This file size should be large enough for important parts of a 50-minute audio session to be shared.

> **Tip**
>
> **Points to bear in mind when sending sound files**
>
> Keep the file size small.
>
> Convert and compress .wav or .aiff or .au files to .mp3 files before sending.
>
> Use a web server such as http://www.pando.com or http://www.sendthisfile.com to send large file attachments.
>
> Send web URLs where favourite music is performed as an alternative to a sound file.

This chapter has discussed some possibilities for using image and sound online therapeutically. It has considered some of the drawbacks and technical issues involved in using computer technology to do this and has provided a brief view of how such technology might be used. By now you may be wondering how online counsellors obtain support and supervision for their work (especially if your own supervisor has declared that they are technophobic). The next chapter discusses this important issue.

Practice activities

For Using Sound and Image Online

1 Visit http://www.therapeuticairwaves.blogspot.com and listen to a discussion about online counselling.

2 If you have a webcam, make a short video about yourself which you could put on your website for visitors to view.

3 Visit Second Life, www.secondlife.com and take a guided tour.

Chapter 8

Supervision Online

Supervision is not necessarily a requirement in all countries for qualified and experienced practitioners. However, it is widely accepted that consultation or supervision helps counsellors to ensure that they are doing the best work they can with their clients. It is a space to reflect on work with clients, and to make sure that neither clients nor ethical issues, or the process between the client and the counsellor, are being overlooked. It must be a safe enough relationship for the counsellor to be able to be open and honest, while enabling challenge and professional development to take place.

The examples in this chapter are taken from Anne's practice and this is to whom 'I' refers in some places.

ONLINE SUPERVISION

There are different ways of understanding the term 'supervision online', which are not better or worse, right or wrong. The first concerns the supervision of *online work*, alongside the usual supervision of f2f clients in an f2f supervision session. Then there is supervision that takes place online *of online clients only*. Lastly, there is supervision that takes place *online to which both f2f and online clients* are brought. Practitioners may find it useful to discover whether there are specific guidelines for supervision of online work from their professional body. For example in the UK, it is helpful to read the BACP Guidelines for Online Counselling and Psychotherapy (2005).

Since working online as counsellors, we have felt it necessary to find an online supervisor. Our fear is that a supervisor who has never worked online may well be unable to provide fully effective supervision for e-counselling, and in some cases may be suspicious of it. It may also be useful to work in the same medium, as it is perhaps easier to spot what is happening in the client work – parallel processes, for example. If your f2f supervisor is sympathetic to e-counselling, but does not work online with clients, we suggest you consider setting up online supervision for that part of your work.

In general, we do not recommend online supervision of f2f clients. However, there may be advantages of online supervision for f2f work. For example, early in my career, I had a very good supervisor, but when I started to work with organizations I had more experience of this than he did. I could not locate another supervisor with the necessary workplace experience in my geographic area. It would have been very useful for me at that time to have found online someone to support this area of my work; they could have been anywhere. Counsellors working in areas where there are few or no supervisors may need to use online supervision. Another case where it might be valuable is where a supervisor or supervisee moves location. Until a new f2f supervisor is found by the supervisee, online work could fill the gap.

One supervisor with whom we discussed this chapter commented on her experience of working online, using email and live sessions, with an f2f practitioner. Although in feedback the supervisee said she had preferred the live sessions, the supervisor found that the emails sent to her made it much easier to pick out which aspects of the supervisee's work were being focused on, and which aspects seemed less important to her.

But what is the professional position with regard to online supervision? This will vary according to where you are. In the UK, for example, BACP accepts online supervision, although there still appears to be a preference that this is for online work only. Online supervision is very appropriate for counsellors who 'meet' their clients in this way. With regard to online supervision for f2f counselling, there does not seem to be a 'rule'. It seems likely that doing what makes professional sense may be acceptable to a professional body if a reasoned, ethically based case is made for supervision in a different mode. In this sense, online supervision is still in its infancy, so you may need to check with your own national body. If supervision is not a requirement in your country, you will not face this dilemma.

HOW DOES IT WORK?

Online supervision works in two ways, although they are not mutually exclusive. It takes place in exactly the same way as counselling online: real-time online sessions or email. For the first format, supervisees might arrange a 'real-time' session, in the same way as they would an f2f appointment. There is then a meeting, either in Messenger or in a dedicated online conference room. Much of what has been said in Chapter 4 about working synchronously applies here. If the supervisee works with clients in real time, then, again, it can be useful to parallel this in the supervision contract, as shown in the extract below. You will notice that question marks are used in some of the supervisor's comments to add a tentative note to what is being written.

> Lisa: may be the new online client. . . .
> Lisa: wondered about how I'd expressed it. . . .
> Lisa: The thing is I wasn't sure she'd read the contract, and I will not always have time to respond on a Friday as I did it in my admin time. . . .
> Lisa: There was a lot to hear in the first email with the contract etc. so perhaps she will have taken it in this time.
> **Anne: That makes sense. . . .**
> **Anne: Hmmm thinking**
> Lisa: Me too!
> **Anne: I notice I'm feeling a bit tentative here. . . .**
> **Anne: I'm wondering if she actually doesn't hear the later parts of conversations, and people get impatient with her and/or say formal/business things to her before anything else, so then she doesn't feel heard at a relational level? (Oops! Too long a sentence. Sorry)**
> Lisa: Lol! to sentence length. Parallel process with what I did in my contact with her.

At the beginning of an online supervision session, as with f2f work, there are often a few exchanges of a general nature, checking how the supervisee is, what their overall workload might be, any current development needs or asking how they have put into practice something we have discussed in an earlier session. Then we establish what is wanted from the session – our goals. If there are a number of issues on our agenda, we often ask the supervisee how they would like to break down the allocated time.

Again, as in f2f work, we highlight when we are coming towards the end of a session. It is also worth checking that they have had what they need from that day's work together and whether there is anything they would like to highlight that we need to come back to in a future session.

Very often, the supervisee will send an email before meeting, stating what is wanted from supervision that session, and possibly attaching extracts from recent emails or Messenger sessions with the client. This is helpful as it enables a focus to be established very quickly in the real-time session. However, as supervisors, we always check that this is where the supervisee wishes to begin. There may have been more exchanges with the client in the meantime, or the supervisee may have moved forward in understanding what is happening. In addition, there could be something more urgent happening with another client. An example of an email sent before a session is shown below.

> Hi Anne,
> Attached is a selection of correspondence with my client.
> My supervision goal is to establish whether my efforts to support Jenny are worthwhile or whether I am wasting my time and hers. As you read you will realize that from the outset I was concerned due to her being in Central America. Once I heard she was 28, I felt reassured, but later she confirms that she has numerous problems, including a possible mental health issue. I also wonder whether she has a learning difficulty.
> She never writes an email longer than this one is now. The MSN communication never happened. Frequently she 'ignores' things I say/suggest. My responses are now short, since her ignoring my trying to establish what she wants from counselling.
> Do you think I should send an ending email or shall I keep the contact going in the spasmodic responding to her bursts that have been are communication pattern since January?
> I would think she has had about 3 hours of my time to date.
> Speak Wednesday on MSN.
> Hilary
> PS Don't feel obliged to read all the attachment. I got carried away. The first two pages perhaps then skim.

The other method of online supervision is solely by email. Vernmark (2005) looked at the benefits of e-counselling, many of which apply to supervision. He suggests that clients like to write when they think about things, and that it is more difficult to go back to thoughts and feelings at a later stage (see also Chapter 4).

In some supervision contracts, counsellors may email a résumé of the client work and/or issues arising. The supervisor reflects and responds. The advantages of this way of working are that the supervisor has more time to reflect before answering, and sometimes the very act of writing the email and re-reading it, enables the supervisee to understand more of what is happening.

When working by email supervision, as with clients, we may write back in a new email or we may write within their text, depending on which seems the most appropriate at the time for that particular supervisee and that particular client.

Below is the beginning of an email attachment outlining what issues the supervisee wished to concentrate on. Comments would normally be in a different colour to the supervisee's, which adds to the clarity when reading my reply. We've used italics in a different font here.

> I have summarized my work and thoughts for your comments:
> * I have 1 client that I have now seen for 3 MSN sessions.
> * I had one person for a one-off email session – she found that helpful and will think about further work – money is an issue.
> * The civil partnership who I emailed you about before I started to work with them.
> Most are Christians – *AS: just checking so I am au fait with*
> *your work – is the bulk of your work with Christians?*

The second extract from the same attachment concentrates on part of our discussion of one client, given the reference GLM. Again the supervisor's comments are inserted in italics, in a different font.

> GML – Australian descent with history of neglect from middle class parents – one was a gambler and the other engrossed in charity work. GML became the main carer (after school hours) of her four younger siblings. GML now late 30s and single. She was raped by an unknown man 2 years ago but said nothing to anyone. She went for counselling at an agency and had 8 sessions with them for PTSD. They discharged her in May.
> *AS: 'Goodness' is my reaction to her being discharged after 8 sessions.*
> *a) I wonder how she felt about that, and b) I wonder what led them to*

discharge her – might she have covered up how she was feeling and let them think she was OK – given that she sounds as if she may cover up her feelings ('said nothing about it' and also possibly there was covering up of the addiction in the family – to gambling and to work)?
We have had 3 MSN sessions.

Concerns: she has had suicidal thoughts since the rape. I made a condition of the counselling that she promised not to harm herself or others while we are working together. In addition I asked for the name of GP; a 'friend' I could contact if I was concerned about her and the name of someone who would support her by phone calls, and cups of coffee etc. She agreed to all of them and I have the evidence. *AS: Excellent – good ethical care of client.* These sessions are going well. She is working on why she gets involved with men who are not good to her. *AS: Possibly this may be something to do with her father – almost trying to replay the childhood situation and 'save' or get love from someone who wasn't good to her, and get a different ending?* On exploration of her upbringing it is amazing that she is as good as she is but she is willing to look at this realistically and is working hard. *AS: Good.*

I feel fairly positive.

Another advantage is that supervisees, by agreement, can use emails for emergency issues arising in between scheduled contact, rather as they would use the telephone in between f2f sessions. For me, this works well, enabling me to give a more considered reply to an urgent matter than when I am caught on the phone, particularly if I have had a glass of wine or two! However, it does mean being clear how often you access emails, and then being rigorous in doing so.

We also use this with some f2f supervisees, who feel confident with using emails, between sessions. An extract of an email exchange with a f2f supervisee, during a period when I was abroad, and unobtainable easily by phone, is given below.

I am aware of:
– her special needs, battling with dyslexia, so having a difficulty with communication all through her life *AS: So really needs a lot of reflecting, summarizing, paraphrasing (all the basic skills) to show that she can communicate with you?*
– her feelings of 'not being heard' when she has complained of bully-

ing (oh, tell me the old, old story – it drives me crazy to hear how many young people feel like this) *AS: Again need for affirming you are hearing her feelings?*
– though she seems 'cold-blooded' in the planning of his fights, she did show emotion when talking about her parents – being 'in the middle' being 'pulled both ways', and she also said it was 'embarrassing' to have problems with reading and writing. I think there is a lot of room for building a relationship – IF she returns. *AS: This sounds a bit hopeful – I'm recognizing the possible parallel in your feelings too – pulled both ways. You feel both pushed away from her by her actions, yet pulled towards building a relationship?*
– I was, however, also conscious of something 'simmering' just below the surface, and felt safety concerns for myself. (Nobody in the outer office: another counsellor with a client, 'covering' for me, but upstairs and out of earshot! – I will raise this with my Controller.) *AS: If she does come back I am adamant that you need to take care of yourself – both for the obvious safety reasons, and also to enable you to relax and be there with her. I'm glad that you are going to check this out, and also wonder if you have a personal alarm. There may also be a need to remind her of two points in the contract if you haven't already done so – there must be no violence in the counselling room, and that also confidentiality may not be able to be held in cases of harm to self and harm to others.*

Obviously these are not either/or ways of offering online supervision. So one supervisee regularly emails background information and an idea of what she would like to cover in our online real-time session, but also does other parts of her supervision solely by email.

A final advantage of online supervision in either format is that there are no notes to be written up by either party afterwards – a full record is there already! The same amount of care must be taken with the storage of supervision emails and real-time exchanges as you would take with client documents.

WHAT ARE THE DISADVANTAGES?

In real-time conversations, typing speed and accuracy (or their lack) can be an issue, particularly if one party has a strong 'be perfect' driver, and feels the need to correct 'typos' (mis-spellings) or use complete sentences.

In such cases, it may feel as if not as much actual supervision has happened as in a f2f session. In our experience, if people allow themselves time to get used to this way of working, these apparent problems disappear. In emails, there may be a perceived need to express things 'properly' rather than conversationally, though perhaps this is no different from f2f supervision where supervisees may present their work fairly formally.

Technology can fail! In my case, this leaves me frustrated, and it can hit an old script of 'I've done something wrong'. It is helpful if emails by either party are acknowledged as soon as possible even if the full response comes later. Our solution is to have a Hotmail address (a web-based free email service: www.hotmail.co.uk) as well as a working address, so that if a computer fails we can send messages from another computer anywhere to supervisees. If connections fail near to a real-time meeting, it is useful to have mobile or landline phone numbers to contact the other person. Very occasionally, the ether does seem to play the role of a spoilt child, and one or other of the participants is repeatedly thrown out of the conversation. This all sounds terribly frustrating, and not worth the effort, but while acknowledging this as a possibility, problems are infrequent. And of course, f2f supervisees can fail to arrive because of some hold-up on their journey.

Confidentiality can be another source of worry, and both supervisor and supervisee must address this fully in contracting, including whether they are choosing to use password protection, secure conferencing, storage of data, encryption etc. In an agency, who else might be able to access data? Often online counsellors in organizations have back-up from IT departments to help ensure internal and external confidentiality. However, protocols to ensure data confidentiality can only be effective where they are adhered to in practice. We do not take confidentiality online lightly, but sometimes it does seem as if confidentiality offline is thought of as secure and online not. This is obviously not so – f2f practitioners sometimes assume that locked filing cabinets are totally secure even if everyone knows where the keys are kept!

One last aspect of confidentiality crucial for online workplace supervision is where the computer is situated. If it is in a family room, or an open plan agency location, then confidentiality is immediately compromised. If we are writing supervision emails, or taking part in real-time supervision, we need as much privacy and lack of interruption as we would have with an f2f session.

In some countries the accrediting or licensing body requires a certain number of hours' supervision per month. The number of emails equating to this requirement, which is of course based on f2f supervision, has to be thought through carefully, and may need revising in light of individual experience. Anthony and Jamieson (2005) draw attention to the need to define what constitutes 'an hour' in online supervision. There will be a need for an agreement about how many emails constitute the equivalent of an hour, and whether an hour online in Messenger is equivalent to an hour's f2f supervision. For purposes of professional accreditation, this will also need to be checked with your professional body.

GROUP SUPERVISION

We have been discussing one-to-one supervision, although at various times we have both also been a part of online groups. Again, this can work in real time, although practice is needed with online group meetings. They can be tricky – or maybe the potentially disinhibiting effect of being online simply makes the dynamics more obvious sooner! If your online training included group meetings, then you will probably find it easier to adapt to group supervision online in real time.

Online group supervision can also be asynchronous, perhaps by email discussion thread. This is where an email is copied to all members of the group, who will add their thoughts to the original, so that a chain conversation takes place. Another way is through a private email discussion forum. Yahoo offers such a facility and has the advantage that it is not accessible by casual browsers, as would be the case in groups that are more public. The issue for discussion is 'posted' on the forum, or notice board, and is also sent round to other members of the group in an email. They reply with their thoughts and reflections which are sent round and posted to the discussion forum in the same way.

Our advice would be to familiarize yourself with working online both with clients and in supervision in a one-to-one dialogue before undertaking group supervision online.

A LIVE DISCUSSION ABOUT ONLINE SUPERVISION

Some issues about using online supervision were highlighted during a workshop. The focus was on training as an online supervisor. We include an extract below, as it gives a sense of the conversation as well as the issues in a more lively way than simply writing about them. You will notice that we have not edited out our abbreviations or sentence structures, since these are what give the 'in-the-moment' dimension to our discussion.

> Kirstie says:
> For me online supervision is both slower and yet more focused which has a faster element
>
> Jacqui says:
> it certainly helps focus my mind on what to bring and what I need – for the moment I think it takes more preparation than I often do when going to f2f sup
>
> Anne says:
> Does that mean it could lose spontaneity J? Or is it of value to prepare more? Or both, may be?
>
> Jacqui says:
> uhm – value to prepare more (which is something I do whenever I am doing something new in whatever field) I still like and need spontaneity so the preparation is not set in stone but a basis to work from and see where it goes
>
> Anne says:
> Makes sense. What do you think , K?
>
> Kirstie says:
> I do prepare more for online. I do think it loses some spontaneity and creativity but it gains in allowing space to focus and really notice the feelings, thoughts that come up as I write or wait for someone else to write
>
> Jacqui says:
> I guess there seems more room for spontaneity in MSN than perhaps there is in emails . . .
>
> Kirstie says:
> I often come to realizations online or aha moments which seem more frequent online than f2f
>
> Jacqui says:
> but I still find I can add spontaneous thought there and then expand
>
> Kirstie says:
> But I also feel sometimes I cover more ground f2f
>
> Jacqui says:

I think the email sup is where the free child is least likely to come out and which can be so restorative at the right moments

Anne says:

just thinking here . . .

Anne says:

as I was sitting back and following your thoughts . . .

Kirstie says:

Well I guess it is the least immediate and the free child is so immediate that it would be so much easier to hide the free child in email

Anne says:

would it be useful if you use the emails and live sessions you'll have together to try to bring in the elements you find most difficult/ most lacking in online work? . . .

Anne says:

so J would look at trying with K's help to get the free child into email sup . . .

Anne says:

while K would go for increasing spontaneity/creativity with J's help . . . for example.

Anne says:

I don't mean at the exclusion of all else, but to keep in awareness?

Kirstie says:

It sounds good.

Jacqui says:

I like that idea – room to experiment

Kirstie says:

I was thinking sometimes with online supervision as sup'ee I do an email so that I get the content out of the way rather than spend my time typing in session. Useful for me but might mean a heavier load on the sup'or

Jacqui says:

I think it is this part where I need to put in the most thought ahead of time so that I crystallize what I really want to explore and not to just tell the client story again

Jacqui says:

remembering that the sup does not need to know all that I know about a client

Anne says:

Agree . . . and that reflecting or writing first can help that?

Kirstie says:

It is often useful for me to have 2 bites of the cherry as it were in that having written an email in advance by the time that I get to online sup I have focused a little more even without consciously thinking about it

Jacqui says:

yes and this is where the self-reflective practitioner part of me works hard

Kirstie says:

Is that the perfectionist part of you as well? I often think it is the perfectionist part of me that gets in my way most in online work. It is something about seeing the words in front of me so that I can notice in advance of sending them how I feel or think about what I have said

Jacqui says:

yes you could be very right here K, I think that it is still perhaps harder to just 'have a go' online as the evidence is in a savable format will keep this in mind as we work

Anne says:

Interesting K – to notice what online work brings out in each of us – could be a help or a hindrance. As a sup/or there's a need to watch out for that in sup/ee as well as in self?

FOR THE FUTURE

Already it is possible to use webcams and voice links. Some of these are excellent and some 'sticky'. (See also Chapter 10 for more information on using these.) Maybe supervision would be a good arena for you to experiment, before using them with clients. In a few years, it is possible that online supervision will be no different from f2f supervision, apart from the physical location of participants. To sum up, we strongly recommend that, particularly in the early stages of your career as an online practitioner, you set up online supervision or consultation. As well as adding to your online experience, it can be a real support to have the opportunity to develop your practice with another online specialist. Online supervision is still a comparatively young field, so there are plenty of opportunities for you to input and influence developments, should you so wish.

Practice activities

I Think of a forthcoming f2f supervision session, and prepare an email stating what you want from the session, as if it was going to be e-supervision. Then write an attachment that you might send to an online supervisor, giving the background to the clients and/or issues you want to discuss.

2 Ask a counselling colleague to act as a peer supervisor with you, and either exchange and respond to supervision emails, or arrange a synchronous session. If it is impossible to find a colleague who will work on the internet, exchange letters with a colleague as if they were emails, in order to carry out the exercise.

3 If your supervisor is amenable and has an email address, you might want to try out supervision by email. You may need to do this a couple of times to iron out any initial problems.

Chapter 9

An Overview of Useful Theories

INTRODUCTION

Online counselling can be practised by counsellors from many different approaches, although we believe that it is necessary to be able to demonstrate the core conditions online in order to establish a working alliance regardless of theoretical orientation. As has been discussed in earlier chapters, the 'disinhibition effect' may mean that many online clients work deeply more quickly, or reveal more of their narrative earlier than perhaps they would working face to face. This is the opposite of 'inhibition', which counsellors may experience with f2f clients, who find it difficult to express their innermost thoughts and feelings initially. There is something about writing to an anonymous person online, that can encourage clients to say much more. This 'disinhibition' can be useful, or may later make them wish they had said less, and so withdraw. Therefore, whatever your own approach, you may need to adapt it in light of this.

It is also the case that many students undertaking training to work with online clients find that they are asking more questions than usual. If this is something that does not fit with your approach, then you may well have to think how you are going to adapt or modify the way you write in order to be more reflective and less questioning. If working by email, you may also find that you are saying more in an email response than you would 'normally' say at any one time face to face.

This chapter discusses several of the major approaches in terms of how they can be used with online clients. At the end of the chapter, the exercises encourage you, whatever your approach, to reflect on whether or how you will be able to maintain your core model when working online.

FOUR EMAIL EXCHANGES USED TO EXPLORE COUNSELLING APPROACHES ONLINE

In order to highlight how a variety of approaches may be used online, an excerpt from a piece of work is used to demonstrate possible responses. This is a fictional excerpt, using an integrative approach, but draws on a number of real client/counsellor exchanges, amalgamated for this purpose. In this chapter, which concentrates on the application of various counselling approaches, little mention will be made of contracting, as we explored this in Chapter 3. The contract would already have been agreed before these therapeutic exchanges began.

Not everything is examined with regard to the approach used, so it is worth noting other points that you spot. You will be able to see many more examples of what you might pick up in the client's emails, and have thoughts about how you would have responded. You might want to note these as you read the chapter.

Very little has been written about using different approaches online. You will also have your own 'library' of texts that inform your f2f work, so use them alongside, or instead of those we have suggested, as these merely reflect some of our own preferences.

First emails

> Anne
> I am finding things a bit of a struggle at the moment and would really like some support from you. I am feeling very frightened and anxious because I have felt low for the past week. I am shocked too as I felt my life was under control now – that does not seem to be so now.
> I have left work early today, saying that I have a cold brewing. It's true, BUT, more truthfully, I just had to get away – I felt close to tears.
> Chris

Person centred-counselling uses the relationship to facilitate the development of the client through the use of the core conditions. Thus an online counsellor will be trying from the first email to show empathy and acceptance. As Trahar (2001) suggests, these qualities in the counsellor will determine the relationship. From this approach, the reply might reflect on the feelings, and wait to see what the client picks up in the next email from what you have written. Thus, you might write:

> Dear Chris,
> Thank you for your email. It sounds as if you are finding things difficult at the moment, and needing some support from me. It must be hard to feel out of control, scared and worried and have been so low for a week now – it's shocked you and made you feel very tearful, so much so that you just had to get away from work. I'm hoping I've heard this right. Do tell me when you reply.
> Warm wishes,
> Anne

The strength of this is that you are not guiding the client in any way, but enabling them to fully set the direction. As in f2f work, the client feels heard and understood. You have also not written more than they wrote to you, so are creating equality in the relationship by not appearing as the authority or the expert on them. However, because of the time lapses between email exchanges, the downside of this might be that the client is left feeling that you are not giving them the support they have asked for in the email. Even in an early email, you might want to add some self-disclosure, which would enhance the sense of support, and add more warmth, such as:

> Chris, I noticed as I read your email that I had a real sense of how anxious you were feeling as you wrote it, and I wanted to be able to reach out and support you.

If a psychodynamic counsellor were responding to Chris, there would be an interest in how the present is informed by the past (Jacobs, 2004). There might also be an interest in the interpretation of written communication as a metaphor. The use of 'now' twice might be noted in Chris' first email – is there a suggestion that life has not been under control somewhere in the past?

Second emails

> Dear Anne,
> Thanks for your email. Yes you have got it right – that is how I am feeling. It's gone on the same all this week too. I have to take myself away from people so they don't know I'm upset. I am back at work as I couldn't go on saying I had a cold, but it's been hard to stay there. At home I am doing the basics, but it's as if I am not really with it – does that make sense? My partner hasn't seemed to notice, thank goodness, and the children are too busy doing their own thing anyway.
> I'm not sure what else would be helpful to tell you. Hope you can help.
> Cheers
> Chris

From a psychodynamic perspective, the core conditions, while useful, are not seen as 'sufficient' as Rogers (1967) contended, and there might be speculation here about the client's earliest attachment. Chris is making sure there is little contact with people, and has an expectation of not being noticed, which could indicate her Internal Working Model. The focus of the next email from the counsellor might well be on the underlying anxieties.

A counsellor working from a Gestalt perspective is interested in helping clients to be aware of their unique perception of how they function within their own systems and environment. Therefore the focus of the response to Chris's email might well pick up her definition that people should not know she is upset, and her sense that it is hard to stay away from work. The object in doing this would be to help her recognize how she might be contributing to her own circumstances, and then help her to consider options and creative new ways of relating. For more on Gestalt counselling, see Mackewn (1996), for example.

In Transactional Analysis terms (Stewart, 2007), perhaps the focus might be on scripts and drivers: is there a 'busy' driver, or a 'never be upset' one? The counsellor might choose to work with these, or keep this awareness as a possibility.

> Dear Chris,
> Thanks for letting me know I had understood what you were saying

correctly. You say that you are taking yourself away from people at work, and it sounds as if that may happen, but perhaps in a different way, at home too. I guess this could be a well tried and tested way of keeping yourself feeling more in control. Is this something you've found useful in the past? It's important that you do take care of yourself when you feel like this, and yet I also sense it's possibly a bit of a struggle.

I'm going to ask you some questions, to see if we can find a way of giving some relief from your feelings. I hope the questions don't feel too much – if they do, let me know and just answer the ones which seem helpful.

Strange question to begin with:

If overnight a miracle had happened, and when you woke up your life was as you wanted, what would be the first thing you would notice?

As you read this email, how are you feeling right now? If you were going to scale that feeling with 0 feeling as low as you have ever felt, and 10 as good as you could ever feel, where would you place yourself?

The other question I'd like to ask you is what it feels like to have to hide away what you are feeling from colleagues and family.

As I said, please don't feel that you have to respond to all the questions if you don't want to. This is a fairly long email – I hope it doesn't feel overwhelming.

Warm wishes,

Anne

Here techniques from a time-sensitive approach are being introduced (Bor *et al.*, 2004) Working online, the counsellor would aim to develop a conversation that has richness and depth, rather than long duration. This underlying online quality lends itself to brief approaches.

If you work from a psychodynamic perspective, you may decide to set clear boundaries, in terms of when you expect to receive client emails, and on what day of the week you will always respond. This is seen as part of the necessary therapeutic conditions for working with any client. You may also prefer to remain more 'unseen' by the client and therefore the tone of the emails given here might be too friendly or familiar for your approach, and would need altering.

However, f2f brief therapists often do not work to a fixed schedule (i.e. a 50-minute session each week at the same time and on the same day of the week). Again, this fits with the way in which many online counsellors and clients work together. If the client wants or needs to write an email today, this can be done without need to hold it until the next scheduled session. This enables much material to be brought into the work which might otherwise have been forgotten or not seen as relevant by the next session. Emails can be long or short depending what 'I' want to tell you, my counsellor, at that time.

If a counsellor works this way, and clients can send emails as and when they wish, it does not imply that the counsellor must respond instantly. Some ground rules/boundaries will have been agreed in the contract before the therapeutic work begins. However, it does give the client freedom, possibly more so even than when using a Solution Focused Brief Therapy (SFBT) approach face to face. After all, a counsellor could hardly work with a contract that accepts that all clients might turn up on the doorstep whenever they wished, and expect to have contact with the counsellor!

We have found that using some of the techniques from SFBT has enhanced our work online. For example, using the Miracle Question (George *et al.*, 1990), or a version of it, can produce very useful and reflective emails in response from clients. Again, it is interesting to note that in some ways, clients may respond more fully than face to face. Often f2f counsellors will prompt a 'thickened' version of the Good Day, for example – 'And what else would be happening?' 'And who else might be there?' 'Would you be doing or saying anything else?' In emails, it is sometimes astonishing to see how much of this the client has already done. Perhaps the fact of writing enables this to happen. The client can sit and imagine or dream, without being distracted by the physical presence of another. In fact, in the case of this 'amalgamated' client, it took a couple of emails to get to that point.

Third emails

> Dear Anne,
> It was really good to get your email and no it wasn't too long. In fact it was helpful and I felt that you'd heard what I was saying and wanted to help me. Right – your questions.
> If the miracle did happen, the first thing I'd notice when I woke up would be that I feel less out of control.
> When I read your email, I'd have put myself on a 4, but since then, I think I've only been on a 2 most of the time.
> What does it feel like to hide what I am feeling? – well, fairly normal I

think. It's what I've always done.

You said that maybe this was a way of feeling more in control, and said that this had been a way of taking care of myself. Perhaps it was, but it feels as if it's not working now. HELP! Any suggestions of what I could do to take care of myself better – this anxiety is making me feel a bit ill at times. My stomach churns and I can't sleep very well.

I'm really looking forward to your next message.

Bye

Chris

In the email above, a psychodynamic counsellor might be aware of a number of things. For example, there is the 'normality' of hiding feelings and the client's possible surprise in feeling heard. The counsellor may wish to explore where these come from. There might be an interest in the ending for several reasons. First, does the last sentence suggest that a dependence is building up, and is this a useful part of the process? Then, what does the 'bye' mean? It could indicate desperation. This possible reflection on the part of the counsellor might be backed up by the client's indication of feeling out of control. Chris also uses capital letters for 'help'; alongside the lower place on the scale, and not knowing how to take care of oneself, what does this suggest? Lastly, could there be a maternal transference or a regression to infant feelings and experiences?

From an SFBT perspective, what enabled the client to reach a 4 on the scale, and what is happening differently when a 2 is experienced? Is there anything the client was doing when on a 4 which could be reproduced to reach a $2^1/_2$ or a 3?

Dear Chris,

I'm glad that you felt I had heard what you were saying and yes, I would like us to be able to help you. Thank you for answering the questions.

You said that if the miracle happened, you would feel more in control. Can you say a bit more about that – what would you and/or other people be saying and doing? From what you say about hiding your feelings, it sounds as if this has been something you've done for a long time, and it's come to feel completely normal for you. I'm wondering if there was ever a time when that wasn't true.

Thinking about your scores, would you be able to tell me what it was that helped you to be on a 4 when you read my email? Then think about those times on a 2, what could you do to get from 2 to $2^1/_2$ – any thoughts?

The churning stomach and not being able to sleep sound difficult for you. Two thoughts here. The first is a practical one – would it be worth visiting your doctor, if you haven't done so already. It's often worth checking out our physical state as well as our emotions, and the doctor may be able to prescribe some temporary relief for you while we work out what else might be causing the anxiety, and how you can reduce it. The second thought is about taking care of yourself. Often when we are anxious, it's hard to breathe properly, and our bodies become tense. So give yourself a few minutes breathing in and out as deeply as you can, and try noticing if your shoulders, jaw and hands are clenched – if so physically tense them even more, then relax them. Other things that might help with the sleeping are having a warm bath before going to bed, and taking time to switch off from the day and do something you enjoy.

Another long email from me – you might want to tell me things which I haven't touched on here when you write back to me. Don't stick only to my thoughts as you are the expert on yourself, though I guess you don't feel that just at the moment.

Warm wishes

Anne

Here, from the perspective of Brief and Narrative therapies, the counsellor is trying to thicken the story. As Speedy (2008) has said, it is the telling of the stories that is of value. They are of no use if they are simply languishing in the ether. The affirmations of the client and acknowledging the difficulties of the churning stomach and sleep pattern again demonstrate the use of the core conditions, while the enquiry about the past would fit more naturally into the psychodynamic approach. The client asked for help, so a more directive counsellor would be comfortable with giving 'tips' and relaxation exercises. There is also a message to the client about their expertise in the hope that this will subliminally reinforce their ability to connect with their inner strengths.

Psychodynamic practitioners might not use the phrase 'you are the expert on yourself', but find a different way of phrasing this. They may also be interpreting the physical reactions as a replaying of a past event or trauma.

Similarly, if your approach is from a Gestalt perspective, instead of (or possibly as well as) homing in on the relaxation strategies, you might want instead to suggest ways of becoming more aware of where in the body the tension was located, in order to gain insight from the experience of the whole person.

Fourth emails

Dear Anne,

It feels as if we are getting moving somehow now. It was a relief to have some practical things to do to help me – guess that's about wanting to be in control again! I really like your long emails. The breathing thing makes sense. I have tried to use it at work, and it's helped me feel less tearful. That's good as I love my work and don't want to feel I am doing a bad job there. Everyone else seems to be so confident. I haven't been to my doctor yet, as I feel silly and don't want to be a nuisance, taking up time when there's nothing wrong with me. But I will do if things don't get any better.

I think if that miracle had happened, and I felt more in control, I would be able to say 'I don't want to do that' or may be 'I do want to do that'. 'No, I can't do that just now'. People seem to think I can do everything just at the drop of a hat whether I want to do so or not.

Have I always hidden what I feel? Not sure. I think there may have been a time when I was little when I didn't, though it's hard to be certain. My Mum shows her feelings a lot, and while people say it's good to show your feelings, I'm not sure as it makes things hard for other people around you. When the kids are upset, I feel inadequate, as I don't know how to put things right for them. It was OK when they were little as I could cuddle them so they felt better, but they are a bit old for that now. (They are 8 and 6) If I share my feelings with my partner, I'm usually told that if I don't think about it so much, it will be OK. And of course, work isn't a place to show feelings, is it?

You asked about what helped me to be on a 4 when I read your email; I think it's that I felt that you cared about what I was going through and that made me feel warm inside for a bit – how pathetic is that?! You also said what helped me to get to a $2^1/_2$, and childish as it sounds to write this, it made me feel as if I was doing something good – I'd achieved a 4. You must think you are writing to a real dope. It made me want to think what I could do to get to a $4^1/_2$ – well, one thing is to re-read your email when I feel down, and may be try out some of the care things you suggest. I might do that tonight.

I shall be watching the inbox on Tuesday for your reply.
Thanks
Chris

There is much in this email that a psychodynamic counsellor might wish to work with. Is the maternal transference becoming more apparent? There seems to be a wish to please the counsellor, and an implication that the client wishes to be well thought of ('you must think me a real dope'). There are definite links back to childhood, and its influence on the present. What type of original attachment was there (Bowlby, 1971)? Is there a hint here of Chris's Internal Working Model of believing that she is silly and a nuisance? Transactional Analysis counsellors might see this as a possible script, with the messages from the past being of interest, including ambivalent messages about showing feelings. There could also be a sense that it would be helpful to work with the client's inner child.

If you use a creative approach with f2f clients (see also Chapters 6 and 7), there is plenty of scope for introducing that here. You could suggest an unsent letter to Chris's partner, or to her Mum from her young self. A photo of Chris as a child could be scanned in (or simply looked at by the client without you seeing it), and she could write about what she sees in the photo and what emotions that evokes within her. She might draw or produce a collage of 'Myself on a Miracle Day' and send that to you. You might reread Chapters 6 and 7 if this fits with how you like to work.

Dear Chris,
Thank you for your email. I'm glad the breathing helps. Did you try out any of the care things as you said, and what was that like for you?
What struck me as I read it the first time was how often you put yourself down. Did you notice that? You used words like 'inadequate', 'pathetic' 'a dope', 'silly'. I'm just wondering if that's the message you give to yourself? That somehow you're not OK? As feedback to you, that's not how you come over to me in your emails. Struggling at the moment with your feelings, yes, but definitely not pathetic etc. I'm admiring of the way you have thrown yourself into our work together and want to get somewhere with it.
I'm going to be curious about some things now – I hope that this will be alright with you. These are just some thoughts of mine, so if they feel wrong or don't fit, please ignore them and tell me I am wrong. I was noticing what you said about your Mum. Could it be that it was hard for

you when she showed her feelings when you were little and that maybe you didn't know what to do? So you hid your feelings? And now your partner maybe doesn't encourage you to show your feelings either?
I'm really going out on a limb here and putting 2 and 2 together and maybe making 5 instead of 4, but I wonder if anything big happened in your life when you perhaps around 5ish? The reason I ask that is because you say that with your own kids, you knew how to put things right for them, but now they are a bit older, you don't.
I'm glad that you were able to tell me what you felt when you read my email. It didn't sound pathetic, but very honest. I wonder if you've realized that you have done one of the things you said you couldn't do? You didn't hide your feelings but told me about them. How did that feel? What helped you to do that?
If you feel like doing it, there are a couple of things you might try out. The first is keep doing the scaling, and notice when you go up and down. What is it that you do that helps you to be up the scale, and how could you do more of it? The second thing is to imagine yourself saying something difficult to someone – maybe 'No; I can't do that right now.' I'm not asking you to actually do it, but choose a real person and real scenario to think about this, and then write down your worst fears about what would happen.
Warm wishes
Anne

Here it can be seen that the cognitive behavioural counsellor is beginning by reinforcing the strategies and techniques suggested in an earlier email, also giving feedback to the client about how they have been experienced, as well as offering some further tasks.. The narrative and SFBT technique of using curiosity is also present. Once again, there are a number of places where the counsellor affirms the client. These could be seen as building a different type of attachment as a means of repairing the original one, to strengthen the ego, or simply as using the core conditions to build the relationship.

If you work from an existential framework, most of the emails above may have seemed far from how you would work with a client. You would be working with the larger question in your mind – how to be with the client as they struggle to find the answer to 'What is the meaning of my life?' (van Deurzen-Smith, 1988). Your focus would be on the best way to reflect on the basic concerns of human beings such as isolation, loneliness, time and fate, and attempts to overcome these concerns through opposites, including love, eternity and responsibility. You would not be trying to change or 'cure' the client, but solely helping them come to terms with life and living.

These exemplar emails do not set out to be a template of 'good e-therapy', and would not be the end of therapy. They have been constructed to help to show how each of us might implement, or wish to adapt our current f2f models. There is no one right way of responding to a client. It is perhaps only by working with clients that we can know what will work best for ourselves and them. This is one of the reasons that we advocate training to work online – it will give you a safe environment in which to begin to discover this. Chapter 11 looks at training in more detail.

Practice activities

I   Think about your own model of counselling – if you already have a written document on this, for example from when you achieved accredited or licensed status, use this instead.

2   How might you expect to be able to use key concepts and techniques online? Do you envisage any difficulties in adapting your model to online work? If so, how might you overcome these?

3   Go back to Chris's first email, and compose a response that is in keeping with your own approach. You might like to go further than this, and drawing on work you have undertaken with f2f clients, compose a series of emails between yourself and Chris.

4   Look at websites developed for clients to use. If there is a demonstration area, try them out for yourself.

Chapter 10

Boundaries and Online Counselling

Now that we have given you an overview of counselling online, this chapter considers some of the boundary issues that arise in online counselling, many (but not all) of which assist the therapeutic work. In the first part of this chapter we discuss how clients can obtain additional support by visiting other websites or using other internet platforms (e.g. self-help programs, public message boards, blogs, mobile phones, audio/video conferencing, virtual reality websites, etc.). In particular we discuss how the internet can be used for:

- additional information;
- additional support from within the counselling relationship;
- support in times of crisis;
- continuing counselling when either client or counsellor is travelling.

In the second part of this chapter we discuss some of the ways the boundaries of the counselling alliance can be stretched through uncontracted contact between counsellor and client, and the ethical issues that can arise when this happens.

USING THE INTERNET AS AN INFORMATION AND SUPPORT RESOURCE

Using the internet as an information resource is helpful for both counsellors and clients. The internet can hold detailed information about many issues which arise during the course of the counselling. For example, the counsellor can obtain information about relevant medical or physical aspects of the client's medical issues and take these into account in the work where necessary. A counsellor might suggest their client find out further information about issues which concern them by conducting their own internet search. Some counsellors may have assembled useful information and web articles which they can email to their clients.

Support for some clients might include suggesting they do any of the following:

■ Visit information websites that focus on their issue to find out more.
■ Complete a self-help program online which uses cognitive or CBT skills such as http://www.moodgym.anu.edu.au and discuss their progress with you, their personal online counsellor.
■ Visit a public message board on a website that focuses on their issue to read and possibly contribute to the discussion there.
■ Visit a website public chatroom that focuses on their issue to talk to others who may be in a similar situation.
■ Visit a website that contains people's weblogs (blogs – online public journals) such as http://www.blogspot.com to read and contribute to the blogs of other people who seem to be in a similar situation.
■ Start their own blog to record their own thoughts and receive messages from other people who read it and who might share their situation.

Some online counsellors research the internet regularly and have an up-to-date list of potentially useful websites that could be sent to clients to address their issues. Others prefer not to make a recommendation themselves but to support clients while they conduct a search, viewing the search itself as part of the therapy. Online counsellors with their own websites may have message boards on their website that they facilitate and monitor. They may suggest that clients join a message board discussion group which they monitor and consists of their past and present clients. As clients become active on the message board they begin the process of detaching themselves from the counsellor while finding others who have worked through similar issues. There is an example of such message board support in the ISMHO (2005) paper.

Any of the methods of support described above can be a useful addition to therapy, providing clients with an opportunity to try something on their own, using the enhanced understanding of themselves that they have uncovered in therapy. Clients can use the internet to put skills into practice experimentally during therapy (e.g. using an avatar to represent them in, say, Second Life), and then report back and refine their new ideas with their counsellor. By stepping gradually away from the counsellor (using the internet for alternative means of support) they can continue to check back with their counsellor when they need to, until they are ready to put their new life skills to work in the real world.

USING THE INTERNET FOR ADDITIONAL SUPPORTIVE CONTACT

As well as seeking information on the internet, some clients contact their counsellors between therapeutic online sessions for additional support. Although this type of contact may be uncontracted, generally it does not weaken the agreed boundaries of the working alliance and is not to be confused with additional contact that does threaten the alliance. Here are some examples of this type of additional support. The following email was received two days after a synchronous session.

> Your words made me think a lot, particularly what we were saying about how I am with my partner and I've written my thoughts down. I'm sending them to you now in this file attachment. I thought you might find time to read them before our next meeting but even if you don't, just writing them down was helpful. I've not seen things as clearly as this, before, you've really got me thinking.

Another example of this additional email contact might be over a task which was discussed in a live session and agreed that it would be a therapeutic homework task:

> I'm trying to do the writing task but I just can't seem to get started with it – I keep running out of things to say after a couple of sentences. What am I doing wrong? Can you help me please?

In an f2f setting, it is unlikely you would receive such contact in between sessions, and some readers may be thinking that responding to such emails would be inappropriate, but the online setting is very different from face to face in this respect. Clients can, and do, seek additional support and help online. They are trying to work on something that is distressing and painful in isolation, with someone they have never met face to face and a timely, brief, supportive contact from their counsellor helps them to feel 'held'. The promptness of their counsellor's response also contributes positively to this feeling of containment.

In the examples above it is good practice to send a response acknowledging the client's feelings but to keep it brief and supportive. In the case of the first client, you may want to respond without specifically committing yourself to finding extra time to read their additional writing. This could be done as follows:

> Hello . . . , I was interested (but not surprised – you were working very hard in our session) to hear that you had been doing a lot of thinking since our meeting. Thank you for writing down and sending me your additional thoughts. If I have time before next week I will certainly read them with great interest.
> Gill Jones

Where there is a query about completing some homework (as in the second example), it may be useful to have additional notes about the task to send out if needed. It can also be helpful to suggest they re-read what has already been discussed in therapy (the transcripts of online therapy are useful here) as a reminder of their mood and the context of the difficulty they are facing now.

> Hello . . . , I had two feelings when I got your email. I was sorry to read you're having a problem with the task but pleased you wrote to me and didn't sit worrying about it on your own. I'm sending you some notes about the task which may help. Sometimes things seem clear when they are being discussed but become difficult to put into practice, especially on your own. Can you remember what our last session covered? My recollection is, we were saying that you have all the skills needed but sometimes you lose confidence in yourself. If you re-read what we said last time, it will remind you how you felt. (If you have deleted the session transcript I can always send you a copy.)

Please let me know how you get on. I look forward to our next meeting,
Gill Jones

Contacts between sessions generally serve more than their stated purpose and can mean the client is finding the online environment a difficult/painful/fearful place to do the work. If you are sending between-sessions messages it might be helpful to use this in the next therapeutic session. A simple enquiry wondering how they are finding online counselling now the work is under way may be sufficient to begin a discussion about feelings of, say, isolation and doing painful work alone. Most clients benefit from such 'here and now' discussions and are able to continue the work once they've voiced their fears. Such discussions also strengthen the online therapeutic alliance.

Practice activities

Write a brief, supportive response to the following email from your regular client:

> Hi, I'm trying really hard not to lose my temper with mother but you know she can be very demanding and sometimes it's impossible. I became angry with her this evening (I know I shouldn't but I couldn't help it, she's so annoying). She wouldn't let me get on with preparing the evening meal, kept on at me to sit down with her and have a chat. Eventually I shouted at her that I was busy and she went quiet after that. Of course I felt guilty then and had to go in and see she was OK and we had a chat of course! (she always gets her own way in the end). Sometimes she just doesn't realize how little time I have to myself. I'm sorry to bother you between sessions like this but I wanted to get it off my chest. I feel better having told you now. See you online next week as usual. K

OFFERING ONLINE SUPPORT IN A CRISIS

Supportive responses are necessary and helpful to the client in times of deeper crisis, too. These crises may include bereavement, or illness of the client or a family member, as well as other unexpected losses and relationship issues. Some clients may ask for help because they are feeling suicidal. Non-suicidal crises can be temporarily 'held' with a timely, supportive response and, if possible, the counsellor can schedule an early session to explore the crisis further. If a client becomes suicidal, they may let you know in a between-sessions contact. In such situations, you have the same choices as you have in an f2f setting. It is a matter of individual competence and preference if you decide to address the crisis within the therapeutic framework you already have, or to recommend your client contacts a suicide service such as the Samaritans online (http://www.samaritans.org). If you do decide to stay with the client while they explore their suicidal feelings, it would be sensible to agree with them what they would like you to do if you do not hear from them, whom they would like you to contact (the police, a doctor, social services, family member or friend, etc.) and when you should do it. If possible, you should get some information about their geographical whereabouts and, ideally, a landline telephone number, if not an address.

A mini-contract could be sent as an email and might read as follows:

> I am very willing to be online and talk with you. I feel that because of our work together, I can support you and such contact could be helpful to you, but we need to agree to some important things first. I will not alert anybody (authority figures, family member or friends) without your prior knowledge but I would like us to agree that if I don't hear from you within a specified time (you say how long) I will contact someone on your behalf (friend, family member, police, ambulance, doctor, you tell me who) in case you have lost consciousness and it is not clear to me that you wish to die. In order for them to be of assistance to you I will need to know where you are now (an address or a telephone landline). Do you think you can supply this information in your next message?

Of course there is no way of knowing (until you need to use it) if the information the client gives you is correct, and if some people are determined to commit suicide, they will, whether or not they are online to you, or have telephone or email contact with the Samaritans. Some counsellors have also handled crisis situations using mobile phone text messages, others have stayed online using Instant Messenger or email contact. An Israeli suicide chat service (SAHAR – see References) was set up by Professor Azy Barak of Haifa University for suicidal Israelis and has been in operation since 2001. In all cases of crisis, whether suicidal or not, you may want to arrange for additional supervisory contact to support yourself.

The internet lends itself to additional contact because of its swift, efficient means of communication. Therapists who work online recognize that for some clients, using the internet for additional, uncontracted contact is a way in which they get their needs met and will address this with the client as part of the therapy. When clients use between-sessions contact as a regular form of support, the counsellor may think it is appropriate to encourage them to seek other forms of support online in addition to their therapeutic contact.

Suggestions for Between-Sessions Contact

- Keep the message supportive but brief.
- Send your response as quickly as is reasonable (the speed of your response is often as supportive as its content).
- Avoid an informal increase in the therapy (re-contract if necessary).
- Keep to the contracted boundaries and re-contract if necessary (e.g. crisis).
- Explore the client's feelings about working therapeutically online at an early opportunity following an unscheduled contact.
- Suggest other websites with discussion forums for additional support if appropriate.

CONTINUING THE COUNSELLING WHEN EITHER CLIENT OR COUNSELLOR IS TRAVELLING

The internet is a very suitable method for continuing the counselling work when either clients or counsellors are travelling. This is helpful for people who regularly spend periods of time away from home, for example workers in the oil industry and people who live abroad for part of the year. Therapy can continue more or less uninterrupted by using the internet to make contact when they are away and attending for f2f sessions when they are at home. Other clients may have chosen a particular counsellor perhaps because of their specific experience or expertise even though they live a considerable distance away. In such cases, online counselling which follows an initial f2f assessment session is a good option with further infrequent f2f sessions as part of the contract (for example one f2f session per month with online contact in between). For those who travel without their computer, such as backpackers or students taking a gap year, online counselling can take place using internet cafés either for email or live session contact with their counsellor (although the latter is not generally recommended, as internet cafés are very public places).

Practice activity

You receive the following message from your client with whom you normally exchange emails on a fortnightly basis. Reply to the email as their counsellor, negotiating how you will treat any between sessions information.

Hi, I've got that promotion at work which means I'm moving to a new office from Monday and I won't be reporting to Sally any longer (you can guess what that means!). It also means I'll be travelling a lot more (hmm, not so sure about that part, don't like being away from home but can't turn the opportunity down). I want to keep our regular sessions going but it will be harder when I'm away. So I'm wondering if I can update you sometimes by email instead of a session? I really find it helpful to write things down and even if you don't reply I know it'll help me to get things out of my head and on to the screen. This new job is exciting — but it's pretty scary, too! See you online next week as usual and perhaps we can discuss how we can stay in touch.

USING OTHER PLATFORMS FOR INTERNET COUNSELLING

Mobile phones are a useful means of making contact with clients since they are usually kept close at hand and can be more discreet in use. If you receive a text or voicemail message from your client on your mobile phone, it is good practice to reply using the same medium since you don't know if your client has access to their email program from their mobile phone. Other ways in which mobile phone messages are useful for online counsellors are as a way of sending reminders about changes to session times or confirmation of session times (although some counsellors may think such reminders interfere too much with their clients' autonomy) or when they experience a technology failure (as mentioned in Chapter 4).

Some people whose typing/writing skills are limited (e.g. by lack of practice or through disability) may prefer to do their counselling using VoIP
internet phone. The most popular program for this type of contact is
Skype (http://www.skype.com). The advantages of such programs over a
telephone landline are that the call is free if it is to another computer (or
low cost if it is to a land line), and the call can be recorded and sent to the
client's computer as a sound file (see Chapter 7) so it can be listened to
again. The disadvantages of these programs are that even with a broadband connection, the sound can become distorted and (depending on the
quality of the connection) disintegrate temporarily during a call. Video
conferencing using webcams (computer cameras) are also becoming
popular now that programs such as Skype and Instant Messenger all have
video conferencing facilities. However, the picture is somewhat jerky and
only suitable for very fast broadband internet connections. Some online
counsellors offer video counselling services, although there is a suggestion
that even with the best-quality sound and image, the fact that the two
people are not sitting together in the same room has implications.
Casemore and Gallant (2007), in their discussion of video supervision,
describe 'a sense of existential loss based on . . . unfulfilled expectation of
what "it" should be . . .' (p. 44). A virtual reality setting such as Second
Life gives a sense of 'presence' that may reduce this sense of loss. A conference member in Second Life can see the other conference members' avatars
as well as their own, all together in the same virtual setting. They can use
live speech during the conference and also use avatar gestures and body
language to support their presence and participation.

Practice activity

You are working as an online student counsellor and your client sends the following text message to your mobile phone.

Hi, im going to c them 2day im panicking can u help?

Write a supportive reply which you can send to their mobile phone

(Note: some phone companies limit texts to fewer than 100 characters including
spaces.)

UNCONTRACTED CONTACT

Some types of uncontracted contact appear to the counsellor to under-mine the existing contractual arrangements between themselves and their client and can set up some transferential feelings that may intrude on the work or may raise ethical issues. This type of uncontracted contact differs from the additional contact discussed above where the client has moved into a crisis situation or needs help or support for a specific issue. Spontaneous contacts that are not part of a prior agreement can some-times blur the boundaries of counselling on the internet and online coun-sellors need to bear this possibility in mind whenever any additional contact is made.

For some online clients, extra emails or text messages on the counsel-lor's mobile phone may be a tempting way to get a higher level of atten-tion from their counsellors. However, such contacts can also disrupt the terms of the agreed contract and counsellors may prefer to let clients know when this is happening in the hope that they can restore the contractual boundaries as we have shown earlier in this chapter. Uncontracted contacts need to be handled thoughtfully if the original boundaries are to be restored. It may even be desirable to change the original terms of the contract to allow for specific additional contacts.

Unscheduled contact can sometimes add new information that the coun-sellor may or may not be able to use in the therapy. Here are two exam-ples of how information gained in these circumstances can confuse the boundaries of the counselling relationship but may also be useful.

1   Bridget received the following email from an online client.

> Sorry, but I have to cancel our session this evening, my husband has just phoned to say he'll be back earlier than usual and I can't work when he's in the house – he'll come upstairs to see what I'm doing and he doesn't know about the counselling. Can we re-schedule for same time next week – he normally works late.

Setting aside the inconvenience to herself for this late session cancellation which she would deal with anyway, this message gave Bridget informa-tion she hadn't been aware of before. The question of whether or not the client's husband knew about her counselling hadn't been discussed and sounded a therapeutically useful area to explore as it could well have a bearing on the work they were doing already. At the same time, Bridget was aware that the information had been offered in an unscheduled contact so she discussed her concerns with her supervisor and looked at the possible consequences of bringing the subject into the therapy herself or waiting for the client to bring it or not, as she chose. After a brief discussion, Bridget decided that as the information had been offered freely by the client, she could use it in their next online session and did so.

2   Mary received an email from a client's wife. The client in question had been cancelling their live sessions recently and updating her by email. His wife said she had found Mary's address by searching through her husband's address book.

> Please can you confirm that X [client's husband] is still having his sessions with you? I think he's having an affair with someone else and he's using the counselling time to see her. I don't want to know what you discuss, I just want you to confirm that he's having counselling. I'm getting desperate with his lying.

Mary had a number of thoughts about this email. Should she answer it? (A different email address from the client's had been given for a reply.) Should she mention the email to the client? Should she ignore it altogether? She discussed these with her supervisor and decided that she would not reply to the email as she could not break confidentiality with her client. Mary and her supervisor felt that if she did respond using the reply email address, she could only say something like 'I would be breaking confidentiality if I either confirmed or denied whether X is in counselling with me.' Both Mary and her supervisor also thought that a reply from her might encourage the client's wife to persist in contacting her with further questions. However, in the light of this email Mary decided that she would discuss the cancellations and, if necessary, re-contract with the client about further cancellations.

In this chapter we have described briefly how other internet environments may be useful in therapeutic counselling online. We have shown some of the ways in which the boundaries of online therapy might be stretched and extended by clients, and how counsellors can evaluate the impact and decide (in consultation with their supervisor if necessary) how to deal with the situation so as to maintain an ethical position whilst restoring the original contracted boundaries. Finally we have considered the importance of creating suitable boundaries for working with online clients who are in crisis.

Chapter 11

Putting it All into Practice

In this chapter, the focus is on 'so that's the theory; how do I start?' We attempt to answer a number of questions that may have arisen in your mind as you read the previous chapters. The first of these concerns training. We draw on the experience of qualified counsellors who then undertook training online in order to gain practice as online counsellors. We examine what they felt they needed to know before they began online training, as well as what they learnt as they undertook the training.

The second part of the chapter focuses on specific issues arising from working online. These include professional indemnity (currently a live problem as many insurance companies cannot offer cover across national boundaries, and clients may not live in the same country or state as the counsellor); awareness of cross-cultural contexts; legal issues; data protection; and country or state regulations of counsellors and how these could cause problems when working online. Because we both work in England, the information we give reflects this. However, we hope that the comments we make will alert you to the issues you need to consider, wherever you are based.

TRAINING

It is our strongly held view that counsellors benefit from undergoing training before working online. Although you may be a very skilled and experienced f2f counsellor, beginning to work with online clients often results in feeling somewhat deskilled. This is a normal part of learning new skills – 'conscious incompetence' – and although it is uncomfortable it leads to 'conscious competence' and then 'unconscious competence'. During those early stages of 'incompetence', it is helpful to be within a safe and supported learning group, working with role-play or volunteer clients who have plenty of other support networks, and with access to feedback and supervision from someone who already undertakes online work. This gives you the opportunity to try out new skills and to adapt to a written form of therapeutic communication. It also enables you to consider if you may need to adapt your own counselling approach and 'way of being' with clients.

> During those first few weeks of training, I felt as if I was back being a raw novice – it was as if my skills had just flown off into the ether! I knew I was being empathic, but did the client?
>
> (Feedback from trainee)

As well as providing the opportunity to learn the skills needed to carry out the therapeutic work, training will also highlight other practical issues such as contracting, working within the occasional difficulties of technological problems, and legal and ethical issues. These are sometimes 'hidden issues' before beginning online work; i.e. they are not in the counsellor's awareness as they have not yet needed to think about them. While training cannot cover every eventuality, it does encourage you to be aware of the main things you need to discover before embarking in this field.

> When my computer crashed, I felt totally alone and panicky – how could I let my client know what had happened, and how would she react? I'd forgotten to include telephone details in the contract.
>
> (Feedback from trainee)

One other benefit of training is that it provides a network for later support with others working online. In a small survey (Jones and Stokes, 2004) of people who had undertaken online training, the majority were still in touch with their colleagues from their training. One summarized the value of this by writing:

> I know that when I am feeling isolated or unsure when working online, that I have a group of guys out there to contact.

Another stated that she had managed to find a supervisor for her online work through the contacts she had made when training to work in this field.

The best medium for training for online work, perhaps rather obviously, is a course that takes place online. Some counsellors will have become interested in this work by attending an f2f workshop on e-therapy, which may have included making use of computers to practise role-plays with other participants. However, good as these are as a starting point, they cannot fully mimic online learning or work with clients. For example, you have already met your role-play client in the flesh, and you have the physical presence of the trainer to help you out with problems as they arise.

Online courses make use of a variety of software packages to provide classrooms, notice boards, discussion areas, libraries of related material etc., as well as using email communication. In a number of courses, you will be part of a learning group and meet online informally outside the course structure to talk about the course and make friendships. Some of the students may well be in other parts of the world, and this helps you think about such practical topics as working across time bands, as well as making cross-cultural themes a live focus. On some, you can also make use of webcams and voice links to see and hear your colleagues.

Most training courses are provided for post-qualification counsellors. Anthony and Goss (2003) are firmly of the opinion that distance learning is not suitable training for becoming a therapist, and furthermore that counsellors need to have adequate experience in f2f work before undertaking online work with clients. Our evidence supports this view:

> If I hadn't been working for some time with clients in a f2f setting, I really don't think I would have been grounded enough to cope with the extra dimension and pressures of [working] online.
>
> (Feedback from trainee)

It is important that you ask yourself some questions before you begin searching for a suitable course, so that you do not waste your time and money. These might include (in no particular order):

- Do I possess the necessary technological skills to work online at this point?
- If not, are there any introductory courses to deal with this, either from an online training organization, or in an f2f classroom?
- Do I want to do this course because:
  - I think it will be a growth area of counselling.
  - I want to increase my private client base.
  - I'm curious about it.
  - I think our organization might adopt this.
- Does a body that is recognised in my country validate the course?
- What does the course include – and does that meet my needs?
- Can I cope with distance learning, and not meeting tutors and fellow students?
- Do I have back-up if technology fails?
- If, having done the course, I decide that online work is not for me, what will my reactions be?
- Do the courses I am looking at seem to provide support if I encounter problems?
- Do I like the sound of the assignments I will have to do?
- Will I get the chance to experience being a client online during the course? If not, is this a cause for concern? (Alternatively, is it a relief?)
- Are there opportunities to undertake more advanced courses if I decide that I want to take my qualifications as an online counsellor further?
- Will I be able to adapt my current counselling model within this course, or is the training in using one particular counselling approach?

You will inevitably have other criteria when choosing a course, so factor these in too. You should take into account that working online as a private practitioner will not necessarily immediately bring in a huge number of new clients. It is still a relatively new area of counselling, and, like establishing any independent practice, it will take time to build up client numbers. If you are hoping for a quick return on your investment, you may be disappointed. You may be hoping to offer online therapy within a counselling organization. If so, it could be worth first ensuring that there are other people who also see this as a possible development. Otherwise, you could feel frustrated after undergoing training and finding that you are a lone voice in the wilderness.

Since this is an innovative area of counselling at present, most current training courses have been established by those who had a passion for developing online practice and moving it more into the mainstream. While we do not wish to discredit courses that are not validated by an accrediting body, you need to consider whether obtaining a recognized qualification is important to you. This may depend on your reasons for undertaking training and your career plans.

Ways of finding out about courses will probably begin with searching in the continuing professional development sections of your professional journal or undertaking a web search for online training in online counselling. You could find articles both on paper and on the web about online counselling which may mention training courses, or you could contact the article's author. Another way is to ask your network of counselling colleagues whether they have any information, or contact your professional body, particularly if they hold lists of training courses. We have listed the website of our own courses and other UK-based training at the end of this chapter, but do research others too.

Once you have found a course, take time to ask as many questions as you need in order to be sure that this is a suitable course for you. You may feel it would be helpful to ask a past student about their experience of the training, and this can often be arranged by email contact. This equates to talking to past students on an open day put on by f2f courses.

There will probably not be an online interview, so most admissions tutors are very happy to answer numerous emails from prospective students. They want it to be the right course for you too. At this stage of the development of online counselling training, most courses are not solely commercial organizations, but established by enthusiastic practitioners, who are also experienced trainers. They do not want disgruntled students who feel they have been misled. So ask away before filling in the application forms and enrolling!

You are not likely to be learning for seven hours, for example, on a particular day of the week for a specified number of weeks to complete the course, as might have been the way you undertook your initial training in a classroom setting. Therefore you will have to think about how you schedule your life and other work around the (possibly) daily task of checking emails, and regularly meetings online. Also, you will be completing course tasks, which may include a role-play with a 'client', and adjusting to time differences if fellow students are located abroad.

Many trainees say that the course seems to take over their lives. This is not necessarily negative feedback, but simply indicates that often the training cannot be compartmentalized into one day a week, with the rest of life going on as normal. You may have experienced something similar on other courses, but the nature of online training appears to intensify this. This intensification can also apply to the dynamics of group or classroom meetings. Trainees find that such practical matters as not being able to type as quickly as someone else, or not having the opportunity to chat informally over a coffee, can lead to all manner of projections and transferences extremely quickly. Add to this the possibility of disinhibition, and here is a recipe for individuals feeling negatively about themselves, about others, or about the course – or all three.

As you read the two paragraphs above, you may have wondered if this is a warning not to undertake online training! To rebalance that perspective, the comments below are from students who have completed their training.

> It was wonderful to know that nearly every time I switched on the computer, there would be someone from the group online to talk to. I loved the group meetings as they were so alive, and I could really reflect on what people had said as their words were on the screen – it also seemed to give me permission to 'talk' to them later about something they had written.

> Once I mastered what time it would be in Australia, it was great to be able to talk on MSN and learn more about similarities and differences in the way counselling is practised there.

> One of the things I have really learned is that most emails do not need an immediate answer. It's OK to take my time and not feel hassled. It's helped me with all my mail, not just from the course.

ETHICAL PRACTICE ONLINE

Throughout the book, we have highlighted some of the issues that may cause concern for practitioners working online. Here we look in more detail at some of these; however, don't rely solely on the information below, as guidelines change over time, and will vary according to your country or state regulations and legal system. Useful starting places for gaining further information are the websites of the International Society for Mental Health Online (http://www.ismho.org) and the British Association for Counselling and Psychotherapy (http://www.bacp.co.uk) BACP have also produced guidelines for UK counsellors. The American Counselling Association (ACA) or National Board for Certified Counsellors (NBCC) are sources for US counsellors. The Australian Guidance and Counselling Association (AGCA) and the New Zealand Association for Counsellors (NZAC) both address some of the issues raised by online counsellors in their respective countries. The Appendix has details of all these websites.

PROFESSIONAL INDEMNITY INSURANCE AND RELATED LEGAL ISSUES

A decade ago, Pergament (1998) stated 'Internet activities challenge existing definitions of legal jurisdiction', and not much seems to have changed since. Here we can raise only some of the issues, and every online practitioner has to attempt to understand for themselves their responsibilities, and how they comply with the law, wherever they live and work.

All counsellors need professional indemnity to protect themselves and their clients, regardless of whether they work face to face or online. While this is a straightforward matter in most instances for f2f work, it can throw up problems when working online. Your first step is to discuss the matter with your insurers and ensure you have their acceptance of online work (if possible) and any conditions or exclusions in writing from them. Iron out any problems before beginning to work with clients online, or you may find that you put off doing so until there is an issue, and then it may be too late.

Indemnity provision may have been covered in your training course, but because you may not live in the same country or state as your trainers, it may have been of a general nature. One option is to contact other locally based online practitioners to ask with whom they are indemnified.

You will probably be covered to practise with clients who live in the same state or country as you do, but some companies specifically exclude working with those outside these boundaries. As you may not know where your clients live, this can create problems. In that case, your contract would need to specify this. In the USA, there are legal barriers to working across state boundaries, and the licence to practise might be rendered null and void if this happened.

Even if you are able to work across continents and the cover remains in force, your contract should make it clear that if a client were to bring a case against you, it would be considered under the judicial system of the country or state in which you are based.

If you normally live in one country but occasionally live elsewhere, check with your indemnity providers as to your position. For example, I (Anne) have a house in France, although I live mainly in England. Sometimes when I am in France for short periods, I continue to work with online clients. I am covered there professionally as my main practice is based in England. However, should I spend very long periods in France, it could be construed that my main residence and workplace was there, and I would have to seek different provision. This is because clients would need to seek recompense under the French legal system rather than English law, and this should be declared in the contract with the client. This may not be true in all cases, which is why it is so necessary to check out your individual position. It is also true that what is the case now may not be so in the future, so you must keep up to date with current law and professional practice.

CONFIDENTIALITY AND DATA PROTECTION

Chapter 4 discussed a number of factors with regard to privacy and confidentiality, including encryption, password protection and the use of a portable key drive. As an online counsellor, you will want to be able to demonstrate both to your professional body and to your clients that you have taken this issue seriously, should there be a complaint, or legal action taken against you. Part of your contract should deal with the issue of privacy, security and data protection, so that clients are not misled into thinking that there are never any risks involved in online counselling. Amig (2001) reminds us that anyone can provide online counselling, and that disclaimers are often ignored or misunderstood.

In order to consider aspects of data protection, we are taking an English perspective. If you live and work outside England, the points made will still be relevant, but will need specific verification in your own country. The Data Protection Act (1998) in England sets out guidelines for the proper safekeeping of other people's records and personal information, so that their privacy is respected. The European Convention of Human Rights (Article 8) states that everyone has a right to respect for his private and family life, his home and his correspondence.

In relation to personal information bear in mind the following points.

■ Personal information is any data that relate to an individual who can be identified and that include any expression of opinion about the individual and any indication of your intentions in respect of that individual.
■ All data that are in paper files are relevant if they fall within a 'relevant filing system'.
■ A relevant filing system is 'any set of information relating to individuals . . . structured . . . in such a way that specific information to a particular individual is readily accessible' (Adamson, 2007).

A 'relevant filing system' includes both electronically stored information and manual systems where they are 'broadly equivalent to computerized systems'. Therefore it is not sufficient simply to transfer everything onto paper, and ensure there is no trace on your computer. Even if you keep unstructured personal notes, you must ensure that the client is not the focus of the information and that the information is not biographical in any way. Therefore your reflections should focus on you and the process of counselling rather than on the client *per se* (Adamson, 2007).

Other data protection principles that could apply to working online concern the length of time that information should be kept, and the rule that it should not be transferred to a country outside Europe. For the first of these, you need to be within your professional body's guidelines as to how long you should keep client records. The second has implications for online work as your emails to a client outside Europe might be construed as part of your stored information about them. You also need to be aware that your clients' rights may be breached if you do not allow them access to their notes. A consideration here is that this could apply to any online supervision you may have received about the work with them.

In England, you must register with the Information Commissioner's office if you keep personal information about clients on your computer, and it is a criminal offence to fail to do this. Since this applies even if you print and delete notes on your computer immediately, this may well apply to any online work such as emails or live sessions, so it would be wise and ethical practice to ensure that you register. There is an annual fee to do this, currently set at £35.

BREACHES OF CONFIDENTIALITY

As with f2f work, there may be occasions when it is necessary to breach confidentiality. The usual 'catch-all' phrase used is risk of harm to self or others. To give examples from England, there may be specific clear instances of 'risk to others', such as under the Children Act (1989), which applies if you are working in institutions such as schools or Social Services. In the case of the Road Traffic Act (1998), you would need to disclose information only if you were asked about the identity of someone you know to have been involved in an accident. In these examples, most practitioners would take it as part of their normal practice to talk this through beforehand with the online client. However, under the Terrorism Act (2002) it is your duty to report your suspicions without notifying your client in advance. The same duty also applies to the Proceeds of Crime Act (2002). If you are aware that your client has retained any monies procured as a result of crime, you must report this to the police, and may not inform the client beforehand, or you will also be committing an offence.

Even with f2f clients, it can feel nightmarish to work through these breaches of confidentiality. Online there are even more issues to consider. You may think it your duty to breach confidentiality, but is the personal information you have sufficient? It could be that you only have the client's email address, and that your client is using a pseudonym. If you are working across national borders, to whom would you disclose information? Indeed, is it essential to do so in their country? Even an apparently simple matter of wishing, with the client's permission, to talk to their doctor about them may not be straightforward if you are each based in a different country, or even perhaps with different parts of one country.

Currently there are few answers to these issues, and online counsellors need to have thought about them sufficiently not to be thrown by them should they arise, while trying to maintain a balance of not being so constrained by them that they fail to provide a therapeutic encounter. Accessing the websites of ISMHO and ACTO, for example, and raising issues of concern, as well as following discussions on the means other practitioners use to resolve dilemmas, may provide some support.

SPECIFIC ISSUES

The first of the specific issues is client assessment for suitability for online work. Your view on how this can be implemented may well depend on whether and how you assess potential f2f clients. Because you do not have any clues from meeting the client in person, such as their physical state, we believe that client assessment has to be rigorous.

You might wish to use a form that the client fills in and returns before a contract is agreed. This might include a version of the Beck Depression Inventory, for example. This widely used form has 21 multiple-choice questions for measuring the severity of depression. You can find various versions of the original Inventory that you can download by conducting an online search using the words 'Beck Depression Inventory'. You may prefer a form that you have developed. This might include questions designed to establish the client's history of abuse, serious self-neglect, violence, suicidal ideation, and whether they are a minor. Evidence of serious risk in one of these categories may indicate that you would prefer to refer the client to other services (Samaritans, doctor etc.) or f2f counselling. This is not to suggest that a client who has suffered abuse or who self-harms, for example, is unsuitable for online work, but simply that you might not choose to work with them.

Working with suicidal clients online is seen by some mental heath professionals as unacceptable, because of the impossibility of using visual and other clues to assess the state of mind. These critics would also say that because communication is by remote means, online clients cannot be given the help they need to access local medical services. Presumably, these are the same criticisms that were voiced when telephone crisis lines were developed. A counter-argument can be offered: some suicidal clients may well share their thoughts and feelings more readily with an unseen counsellor than in f2f situations, and therefore are more likely to find help. You might also like to reflect on whether suicidal clients who email us are more or less likely to act on suicidal thoughts if refused online support.

The Samaritans' organization offers an email response to suicidal clients, although there is a time delay in responding to emails. SAHAR is an internet-based support system for people in Israel contemplating suicide. Unlike the Samaritans' provision, SAHAR provides synchronous contact with trained responders, as well as written information and links to other sites. It is a free service with high usage; however, it is only available in Hebrew (Barak, 2001).

Since clients can contact you from anywhere in the world, cross-cultural issues may be a feature of your online work. Because you cannot see your client, there could be a danger of ignoring these. Perhaps a starting point is to check your client's understanding of what counselling or therapy actually entails. There are wide global differences in these that may lead to a misunderstanding or misconstruing of the process by either of you. Counsellors either have to be prepared to try to discover sources that will help them understand a different culture (these sources of course could include the client), or restrict themselves to working with clients from cultures which they can be reasonably confident of understanding. Writing about Western diplomacy and psychology, Rifkind (2007) stresses the importance of listening and of not reacting through a Western lens. Although she is not writing about online work, her words are equally applicable here. In the same journal, Wright (2007), in talking about working within the Maori culture in New Zealand, notes that 'the drawback of over-sensitivity to cultural differences is a kind of frozen watchfulness'. Yet again the keyword would seem to be balance – not avoiding the challenge of working with online clients simply because they and you are from different cultural backgrounds, but remaining mindful of the lack of understanding you may have, and referring clients on if necessary.

In concluding this chapter we are aware that you may feel pessimistic about the problems that could beset you in working online, so perhaps it is worth recording the words of a client. These have been slightly altered to ensure anonymity, but the sense has been retained.

> When I first contacted you, I felt desperate, and the fact that you lived 6000 miles away did not help that feeling. How could you understand me and my problems, sitting in your room in England? But because I was desperate, I decided to give it a go. I think it helped that you picked that up and you said to look as well for local support. That help, together with the emails we exchanged, have made a big difference to me – I want to go on with my life now. Thank you.

SO FINALLY – WHERE NEXT?

Technology is developing so fast that it is difficult, if not impossible, to keep ahead and spot a developing trend. Apart from a growth in individual online counselling, we have noticed the trend (particularly with the growth in Web 2.0) for increased interactivity. One trend may be for online counsellors to increase their use of interactive information websites in their work with clients, suggesting that the client views and/or completes specific web-based tasks and then uses the counselling session to discuss their response to the task and their learning from it.

Other areas for development might include:

- Group therapy and group supervision on the internet, using conferencing facilities such as those provided in Second Life.
- Therapeutic podcasts – discussing general counselling issues which are intended to both educate and inform the listener.
- Counselling as 'infotainment' – where fictitious scenarios both educate and entertain. These could be 'video-soaps' similar to those on YouTube but with the addition of specific themes to promote psychological health and well-being.

Whatever the next developments turn out to be, we hope that you will enjoy being part of this exciting world.

Practice activities

1 What would you want from online training? (e.g. teaching sessions, role-plays, supervision of practice). Divide your list into those things that are essential for you, and those you 'might like'.

2 Research online training organizations and check whether they fit the criteria you have drawn up.

3 Contact your professional body and ask them for any guidelines on online counselling. Once you have read them, consider how they may affect your practice. If you are already working online, do you need to alter the way you work in light of these guidelines?

Appendix

Codes of Practice Relating to Online Therapy

We have included here a list of websites where ethical and practice codes specific to the delivery of online therapy can be viewed. We have not attempted to provide an exhaustive list since every country where therapists practise will have its own codes.

CODES AND GUIDELINES FOR UK COUNSELLORS

ACTO Association for Counselling and Therapy Online Code of Ethics and Practice available from http://www.acto-uk.org/codeofethics.htm, accesssed 5 January 2008.

BACP Guidelines for Online Psychotherapy with Guidelines for Online Supervision, by K. Anthony and A. Jamieson, Rugby: BACP, 2005.

Data Protection Act 1998 for more information visit http://www.ico.gov.uk date accessed 5 January 2008.

GENERAL PRACTITIONER CODES THAT ARE NOT COUNTRY SPECIFIC

HON Health On the Net. For more information visit http://www.hon.ch/HONcode/Conduct.html date accessed 5 January 2008

ISMHO Suggested Principles for the Provision of Mental Health Services. For more information visit http://www.ismho.org/suggestions.html, accessed 5 January 2008.

OTHER COUNTRIES' PRACTITIONER CODES

ACA American Counselling Association. The ACA 1999 web counselling code can be viewed at http://www.angelfire.com/co2/counseling/ethical.html, accessed 3 April 2008.

AGCA Australian Guidance and Counselling Association has guidelines for setting up an online counselling service in schools. See http://mhws.agca.com.au/onlcoun_home.php, accessed 3 April 2008.

HIPAA Health Insurance Portability and Accountabillity Act 1996 (for US practitioners, e.g. psychologists who work for medical insurance companies) for information on electronic transfer of data visit http://www.hipaadvisory.com/REGS/HIPAAprimer.htm, accessed 5 January 2008.

NBCC National Board for Certified Counselors. 'The Practice of Internet Counselling' is displayed in full at http://www.nbcc.org/webethics2, accessed 3 April 2008.

NZAC New Zealand Association of Counsellors. Code of Ethics addresses electronic communication. See http://www.nzac.org.nz/ethics/13.html, accessed 3 April 2008.

References and
Further Reading

Adams, K. (1990) *Journal to the Self*, New York: Warner Books.

Adamson, K. (2007) Unpublished notes from workshop on The Law and the Therapist.

Amig, S. (2001) 'Internet Dilemmas', *Behavioral Health Management*, **21**(3), 48–51.

Anthony, K. (2003) 'Email and Internet Relay Chat', in S. Goss and K. Anthony (eds) *Technology in Counselling and Psychotherapy: A Practitioner's Guide*, Basingstoke and New York: Palgrave Macmillan.

Anthony, K. and Jamieson, A. (2005) *Guidelines for Online Counselling and Psychotherapy*, 2nd edn, Rugby: BACP.

Barak, Azy (2001) 'Psychology and the Internet', paper presented at a conference of the British Psychological Society, November. See http://www.constuct.haifa.ac.il/-azy/saharo2.htm, accessed 8 August 2007.

Bayne, R., Horton, I., Merry, T. and Noyes, E. (1998) *The Counsellor's Handbook*, Cheltenham: Stanley Thornes.

Bloom, J. (1998) 'The ethical practice of Webcounselling', *British Journal of Guidance & Counselling*, **26**(1), 53–9.

Bolton, G. (1995) 'Taking the Thinking out of it: Writing – a Therapeutic Space', BACP, *Counselling*, **6**(3), 215–17.

Bolton, G., Howlett, S., Lago, C. and Wright, J. (eds) (2004) *Writing Cures*, Hove and New York: Brunner-Routledge.

Bor, R., Gill, S., Miller, R. and Parrot, C. (2004) *Doing Therapy Briefly*, Basingstoke and New York: Palgrave Macmillan.

Bowlby, J. (1971) *Attachment and Loss*, London: Penguin.

Casemore, R. and Gallant, M. (2007) 'Supervision: Viewed from a Distance', *Therapy Today*, **18**(10), 44.

Chechele, P. and Stofle, G. (2003) 'Individual therapy online via email and Internet Relay Chat', in S. Goss and K. Anthony (eds), *Technology in Counselling and Psychotherapy: A Practitioner's Guide*, Basingstoke and New York: Palgrave Macmillan, pp. 39–58.

Coren, A. (2001) *Short-Term Psychotherapy: A psychodynamic approach*, Basingstoke and New York: Palgrave Macmillan.

Crouch, A. (1997) *Inside Counselling: Becoming a Professional Counsellor*, London: Sage.

Derrig-Palumbo, K. and Zeine, F. (2005) *Online Therapy: A Therapist's Guide to Expanding your Practice*, New York and London: W.W. Norton & Co.

van Deurzen-Smith, E. (1988) *Existential Counselling in Practice*, London: Sage.

Egan, G. (1994) *Exercises in Helping Skills*, Pacific Grove, CA: Brookes Cole.

Evans, J. (2007) 'A Guide to Online Counselling in a University or College Setting', *AUCC Journal*, Winter.

Fenichel, M. (2007) *Here and Now in Cyberspace*, http://www.fenichel.com/herenow.shtml, accessed 10 November 2007.

Fenichel, M., Suler, J., Barak. A., Zelvin, E., Jones, G., Munro, K., Meurier, V. and Walker-Schmucker, W. (2002) 'Myths and Realities of Online Clinical Work', *CyberPsychology and Behaviour*, 1 October, pp. 481–97.

George, E., Iveson, C. and Ratner, H. (1990) *Problem to Solution*, London: BT.

Goss, S. and Anthony, K. (2003) *Technology in Counselling and Psychotherapy: A Practitioner's Guide*, Basingstoke and New York: Palgrave Macmillan.

Goss, S., Anthony, K., Jamieson, A. and Palmer, S. (2001) *Guidelines for Online Counselling and Psychotherapy*, Rugby: BACP.

Hales, J. (2006) 'Computer Therapy', *The Journal of the Association for University and College Counselling*, Winter.

Hudson, J. (2002) 'Community Care in the Information Age', in B. Bytheway (ed.), *Understanding Care, Welfare and Community: A Reader*, London: Routledge.

International Society for Mental Health Online (ISMHO) *Assessing a*

Person's Suitability for Online Therapy, available from http://www.ismho.org/casestudy/ccsgas.htm, accessed 26 November 2007.

ISMHO (2005) *ISMHO Clinical Case Study Group: Half a Decade of Online Case Study*, available from http://www.ismho.org, accessed 2 January 2008.

Jacobs, M. (2004) *Psychodynamic Counselling in Action*, 2nd edn. London: Sage.

Jones, G. (2002) 'Engaging the Client', unpublished email discussion group.

Jones, G. (2004) *Online Counselling: Old Skills in a New Environment*, http://www.gjcounselling.co.uk/trainingonline.htm, accessed 4 January 2008.

Jones, G. and Stokes, A. (2004) 'An Unpublished Survey of Past Students', conducted online for Online Counselling Ltd.

Jones, G. and Stokes, A. (2005) *An Example of Brief Email Therapy Client Marcia: Counsellor Chris*, http://www.gilljones.net/downloads/marcia.pdf, accessed 4 January 2008.

Kanani, K. and Regehr, C. (2003) 'Clinical, ethical, and legal issues in e-therapy', *Families in Society: The Journal of Contemporary Human Services*, 84(2), 155–62.

Kasket, E. (2003) 'Online Counselling: Some considerations for existential-phenomenological practitioners', *Journal of the Society of Existentialist Analysis* 2006 Vol 14 Issue 1 60 – 66.

King, R., Bambling, M., Lloyd, C., Gomurra, R., Smith, S., Reid, W. and Wegner, K. (2006) 'The motives and experiences of young people who choose the internet instead of face-to-face or telephone counselling', *Counselling and Psychotherapy Research*, 6(3) 169–74.

Kraus, R., Zack, J. and Stricker, G. (2004) *Online Counselling: A Handbook for Mental Health Professionals*, San Diego, CA and London: Elsevier Academic Press.

Mackewn, J. (1996) *Modern Gestalt in Counselling: The BAC Reader*, London: Sage.

Malchiodi, Cathy A. (2000) *Art Therapy and Computer Technology: A Virtual Studio of Possibilities*, London: Jessica Kingsley.

McLeod, J. (1997) *Narrative and Psychotherapy*, London, Thousand Oaks, CA and New Delhi: Sage.

Milner, J. and O'Byrne, P. (2002) *Brief Counselling: Narratives and Solutions*, Basingstoke and New York: Palgrave Macmillan.

Munro, K. (2006) 'On-line therapy: the faceless cure?', *Saturday's Globe and Mail*, Toronto, 23 April. See http://www.theglobeandmail.com, accessed 9 August 2007.

Munro, K. *Resources for healing*, http://www.kalimunro.com, accessed 8 August 2007.

Murphy, Lawrence J. and Mitchell, Dan L. (1998) 'When Writing Helps to Heal: E-mail as Therapy', *British Journal of Guidance and Counselling*, **26**(1), 12–21.

Payne, M. (2000) *Narrative Therapy*, London, Thousand Oaks, CA and New Delhi: Sage.

Pergament, D. (1998) 'Internet psychotherapy: Current status and future regulation', *Journal of Law Medicine*, **8**(2), 233–80.

Progoff, I. (1992) *At a Journal Workshop*, New York: Penguin Putnam.

Reynolds, D., Stiles, W. and Grohol, J. (2006) 'An investigation of session impact and alliance in internet based psychotherapy: preliminary results', *Counselling and Psychotherapy Research*, **6**(3), 164–8. See http:www.slais.ubc.ca/courses/libr500/03/04/www/NAnderson/history.htm.

Rifkind, G. (2007) 'Western Diplomacy and Psychology', *Therapy Today*, **18**(9), 12–15.

Robbins, Sarah and Bell, Mark (2008) *Second Life for Dummies*, Indianapolis, IN: Wiley Publishing.

Rogers, C. (1967) *On Becoming a Person: A Therapist's View of Psychotherapy*, London: Constable.

SAHAR – for further information visit: http://focus.haifa.ac.il/spring-2005/02–sahar.htm, accessed 20 November 2007.

Sampson Jr, J. P., Kolodinsky, J. and Greeno, B. P. (1997) 'Counseling on the information highway: future possibilities and potential problems', *Journal of Counseling and Development*, **75**(3), 203–11.

Second Life – for further information visit http://www.secondlife.com, accessed 20 November 2007.

Sills, C. (2006) *Contracts in Counselling and Psychotherapy*, London: Sage.

Silverstone, Liesl (1997) *Art Therapy the Person Centred Way: Art and the Development of the Person*, London: Jessica Kingsley.

Speedy, J. (2008) *Narrative Inquiry & Psychotherapy*, Basingstoke and New York: Palgrave Macmillan.

Stebnicki, M. and Glover, N. (2001) 'E-supervision as a complementary approach to traditional face-to-face clinical supervision in rehabilitation counselling: problems and solutions', *Rehabilitation-Education*, **15**(3), 283–93.

Stewart, I. (2007) *Transactional Analysis Counselling in Action*, 3rd edn., London: Sage.

Stokes, A. (2006) 'Supervision in Cyberspace', *Counselling at Work*, **51**, 5–7.

Suler, J. (1998) *The Psychology of Cyberspace: Email communication and relationships*, http://www.rider.edu/~suler/psycyber/emailrel.html, date accessed 9 November 2007.

Suler, J. (2001) *The Psychology of Cyberspace: Online disinhibition*, http://www.rider.edu/~suler/psycyber/disinhibit.html, accessed 4 January 2008.

Suler, J. (2004) 'The online disinhibition effect', *CyberPsychology and Behavior*, **7**, 321–6.

Thorne, B. (1992) *Carl Rogers*, London, Thousand Oaks, CA and New Delhi: Sage.

Trahar, S. (2001) 'Theoretical perspectives' in S. Aldridge and A. Rigby (eds) *Counselling Skills in Context*, London: Hodder and Stoughton.

Trower, P., Casey, A., Dryden, W. and Fokias, D. (2005) *Cognitive Behavioural Counselling in Action*, London: Sage.

Vernmark, K. (2005) 'Therapy by email', http://www.psychologyspace.com, accessed 16 October 2007.

Warren, Bernie (1984) *Using the Creative Arts in Therapy*, London and New York: Routledge.

Weiser, Judy (1999) *Photo Therapy Techniques: Exploring the Secrets of Personal Snapshots and Family Albums*, Vancouver: Photo Therapy Centre.

White, M. and Epston, D. (1990) *Narrative Means to Therapeutic Ends*, New York and London: W.W. Norton & Co.

Wright, J. (2002) 'Online counselling: learning from writing therapy', *British Journal of Guidance and Counselling*, **30**(3), 285–98.

Wright, J. (2003) 'Future therapy stories', *Counselling and Psychotherapy Journal*, **14**(9), 22–3.

Wright, J. (2004) 'Words, writing about experience and reading other people's diaries', *Counselling and Psychotherapy Journal*, **15**(10), 16–17.

Wright, J. (2007) 'Bi-culturalism and Migration', *Therapy Today*, **18**(9), 23.

WEBSITES

http://www.acto-uk.org (Association for Counselling and Therapy Online)
http://www.befrienders.org
http://cuinfo.cornell.edu/Dialogs/EZRA
http://www.ismho.org
http://www.kateanthony.co.uk
http://www.online-supervision.net
http://www.onlinetrainingforcounsellors.co.uk
http://www.samaritans.org
http://www.secondlife.com

Index